DATE DUE			

The Story of the U.S. Cavalry

"A Fight for Water," by Charles Schreyvogel

The Story of the U.S. Cavalry

1775 – 1942

by

MAJOR GENERAL JOHN K. HERR
U.S.A. (Retired). Last Chief of Cavalry

and

EDWARD S. WALLACE

With a Foreword by

General Jonathan M. Wainwright
U.S.A. (Retired)

BONANZA BOOKS

New York

This 1984 edition is published by Bonanza Books, distributed by Crown Publishers, Inc.,
by arrangement with Little, Brown & Company, Inc.

Manufactured in the United States of America

Library of Congress Cataloging in Publication Data

Herr, John K.
    The story of the U.S. cavalry, 1775–1942.

    Reprint. Originally published: Boston : Little,
Brown, c1953.
    Bibliography: p.
    1. United States.   Army.   Cavalry—History.
I. Wallace, Edward S. II. Title.
UA30.H47   1984   357′.1′0973   84-12350
ISBN: 0-517-455293

h g f e d c b a

Authors' Note
and Acknowledgments

First of all, the authors want to admit, freely and fully, that this book is in no sense a comprehensive history. It couldn't be, and there are gaps and omissions through which a cavalry regiment in line could easily ride. A complete account of the activities of the numerous splinter detachments of our mounted service which were scattered over our frontier for years would fill several tomes. The authors have simply tried to hit the high spots and to light up, a little, the past glory and glamor of the men on horseback.

Many persons have been very helpful and the authors particularly want to thank the following:

Dr. Sidney Forman of the United States Military Academy Library; Mrs. John Nicholas Brown of Providence, R. I.; Mr. Archibald Hanna of the Yale University Library, New Haven, Connecticut; Mr. Thomas Little and Mr. Thomas F. O'Connell of the Harvard College Library, and Miss Carolyn E. Jakeman of the Houghton Library, all of Cambridge, Massachusetts; Mr. Sylvester Vigilanti of the New York Public Library; Miss Margaret Hackett of the Boston Athenaeum, and Mr. Charles Childs of the Childs Gallery, of Boston, Massachusetts; Colonel Martin L. Crimmins, Colonel H. C. Larter, Jr., and Colonel Harry M. Henderson of San Antonio, Texas; Mr. Pat Patterson of the Woolaroc Museum, Bartlesville, Oklahoma; the Anheuser-Busch Company of St. Louis, Missouri; and Mr. Carl E. Stange

Authors' Note and Acknowledgments

of the Library of Congress, and Mr. Thomas Rhea of the National Archives, of Washington, D. C. A special commendation is given to Miss Sherry Hawkins of Boston, Massachusetts, for her extreme patience and good nature, far beyond the line of duty, in the typing and correcting of an often-revised manuscript.

Foreword

This book by Major General John K. Herr, U.S.A., Retired, the last Chief of Cavalry, and Mr. Edward S. Wallace, recounts the history of American cavalry from the Revolutionary War, 1775 to the year 1942. During the Revolution and in all the wars of the Republic since, cavalry has gloriously and nobly served. While the peculiar characteristics of mounted cavalry, in its ability to operate over any terrain, in any weather, and at night, have to some extent been taken over by armored troops and the air force for purposes of reconnaissance, the cavalry must be considered superior to the air force in bad weather, at night, and in heavily wooded country. Off the roads and in mountainous country, armored troops usually cannot operate, and the horseman can go anywhere.

Perhaps the undersigned is the last senior commander to employ mounted cavalry in action against an enemy. In my withdrawal from the Lingayen Gulf in North Luzon to the Bataan Peninsula, under orders of higher authority, the 26th Cavalry, the last regiment of regular army cavalry to be employed mounted in war, splendidly covered the withdrawal of my corps of four Philippine army divisions. This it did at great sacrifice to itself. About 75 per cent of its American officers were casualties and 50 per cent of its Philippine scout soldiers were disabled or killed. Without this gallant little band of horsemen, I doubt if I could have successfully made that withdrawal.

Long have I advocated the retention of at least one full-strength mounted cavalry division, equipped with pack artillery (75 mm. mountain howitzer) which may be carried in pack or drawn behind horses. Such a cavalry division can operate in any weather, in any country, in any climate, and in any terrain. Let us remount the First Cavalry Division and return it to the United States to serve as a nucleus for expansion, if necessary, or for immediate action in an emergency.

JONATHAN M. WAINWRIGHT
GENERAL, U.S.A., RETIRED

San Antonio, Texas

Contents

The Story of the U.S. Cavalry

CHAPTER I

The Early Days
1775 – 1832

At the outbreak of the Revolutionary War, the people of the American colonies were far more dependent on the horse for transportation than we of the United States are today upon the automobile. Unless one walked, or went by oxcart, it was the only way to travel by land. Doctors, lawyers, ministers, farmers and planters, and peddlers and merchants, all rode about their business on horseback and their womenfolk rode sidesaddle or on pillions. In the towns, and where the few good roads existed, people could travel in coaches or other horse-drawn vehicles but the great majority went on horseback. Our ancestors were a nation of horsemen, and the horses, especially in Virginia, were of fairly good breed.

The horse, however, had played only a minor part in our Colonial wars with the Indians and French because the heavily forested wilderness had prevented any cavalry action. The Indians of the East were not horsemen and, against them and their French allies, horses were used only as draft or pack animals by the British-Colonial forces, on the primitive roads and trails cutting through the dense woods to the north and west.

After Lexington and Concord, George Washington took command of the Continental forces in Cambridge in June, 1775. A good horseman and an enthusiastic fox hunter himself, he shared his countrymen's love of the horse and their complete ignorance of its proper use in warfare. His experience in the catastrophic Braddock campaign of 1755, in which no cavalry could be used on the wilderness trails, had given him no cavalry experience and he did not comprehend its value at first. The horses, horsemen, and forage were there in 1775 and an open countryside to use cavalry in, especially between New York and Philadelphia; but the mounted service was not properly used until the southern campaigns near the end of the war. The leaders were there too, for Daniel Morgan and Benedict Arnold had all the earmarks of dashing commanders of irregular cavalry, but they remained on foot, and the war dragged on for over six long years. Fortunately the British, in turn, had the same blind spot and did not add cavalry to their superiority in artillery, infantry, and general equipment.

During the siege of Boston in 1775–1776 the Americans had no cavalry but the British landed one regiment from Ireland, the 17th Dragoons, which was ineffective at the time because many of their horses had died on the voyage. Later this regiment merged with the 16th Dragoons and took the name Queen's Dragoons and did good service with Banastre Tarleton in the South.

After the British evacuated Boston in March, 1776, the main theater of warfare moved to the area between New York and Philadelphia, where it remained until 1778. Before the Battle of Long Island in August, 1776, a regiment of Connecticut "Light Horse" about four hundred strong, composed of men "of reputation and property," reported for duty to Washington. These men had enlisted with the understanding that they would be exempt from guard duty, kitchen police, and other fatigue details because of the extra time needed for the care of their horses and they refused to waive these exemptions and act as infantry. Washington wanted the men but not the horses and finally, fearing that these special exemptions would be bad for the discipline and morale of the rest of his army, he sent them home. In the ensuing battle the British flanked a wing of the American army by a surprise attack and inflicted a major defeat, which was nearly disastrous.

Charles Francis Adams in his essay "Washington and Cavalry" takes the general to task and intimates that the use of these available cavalrymen might have stopped the British, saved New York, and possibly shortened the war by years. But it must be said for the great Washington that he soon changed his opinion about cavalry and became increasingly aware of its value, and his correspondence during the rest of the war showed his strong desire to develop this neglected arm.

First known pictures of American cavalrymen

From Allgemeines Historisches Taschenbach (*Berlin 1784*). *Mrs. John Nicholas Brown*

The lessons of Long Island, and of succeeding defeats around New York were so obvious that Congress in 1777 authorized the formation of four regiments of dragoons which were modeled on the European pattern: not so heavy as armored cuirassiers, but more solid than the light lancers or hussars who depended on the saber and lance for weapons. These regiments were each composed of six troops with a total authorized strength of 279 men and officers. They were armed with heavy sabers and flintlock pistols carried in saddle holsters, and, when available, with carbines, but these were so scarce that a fully armed American dragoon was a rarity. Only native Americans of known stability and proved loyalty were enlisted and this body of light cavalry became an elite corps — at least on paper.

The four regiments popularly bore the names of their colonels; the 1st Continental Regiment of Light Dragoons was called Bland's, or the Virginia Horse, from their native state; the 2nd Dragoons were Sheldon's from Connecticut; the 3rd were Baylor's, mostly from the horsy districts of Virginia and Maryland; and the 4th were Moylan's from Pennsylvania and Maryland, in which regiment served Captain Zebulon Pike, father of the famous explorer of the West. Their uniforms varied. On the fashion plates drawn for models, they all wore buckskin breeches and top boots, but each regiment had distinctive waistcoats and coats of contrasting colors of red, white, blue, brown, or green, with the coats faced with still another of these colors. Their helmets were of brass with a strip of bearskin running down the middle fore and aft. The uniforms were gorgeous but, alas, they seldom clothed a dragoon. Usually the men were dressed in rags and tatters, captured British uniforms, blankets, and even cut-up tablecloths, and the possessor of a pair of boots was a proud and wary man.

*Count Casimir Pulaski, first commanding officer
of American cavalry*

The first commander of this cavalry corps was a dashing
young Polish nobleman, Count Casimir Pulaski, whose estates
had been confiscated by the Russians and who had come to
America by way of Turkey and Paris to offer his services to
Washington. He was zealous in his duties but spoke no English
and knew nothing about local customs or the terrain, and his

7

subordinates resented this exotic foreigner. Pulaski resigned in March, 1778, to recruit and lead his famous "Cavalry Legion," a mixed body of horse and foot largely composed of foreign officers and Hessian deserters. He died gallantly charging the British artillery at Savannah in 1779.

Pulaski was succeeded by an engaging Irishman, Stephen Moylan, who had commanded the 4th Dragoons, and who was every bit as colorful as his predecessor. Moylan was born in Cork, Ireland, in 1737, the son of a wealthy merchant and the Countess of Limerick, and was educated on the Continent, probably in Portgual, as were so many young Irishmen of good family of that time, because of the British restrictions against the education of Roman Catholics. He came to Philadelphia in 1768 where his background and breeding gave him an entree into the best society, and where he became the first president of The Friendly Sons of St. Patrick.

Moylan's friendliness, however, had not extended to his commanding officer, for he had quarreled with Pulaski, and had subsequently tilted with lances with a subordinate Polish officer, in which joust the Irishman was unhorsed. Moylan's temperament may be gauged by his comment on the Battle at Princeton: "I know I never felt so much like one of Homer's Deities before. We trod on air — it was a glorious day." His regiment had been clothed for a while in captured British uniforms of red waistcoats and coats, but he soon replaced the coats with ones of emerald green, "the green over the red." This handsome uniform and "his merry nature and fine appearance" won the heart of a New York heiress, Mary Ricketts Van Horne, whom he married in 1778.

Unfortunately these dragoon regiments were handicapped by lack of equipment, and the few properly mounted and armed

men spent most of their time on duty at Washington's headquarters as couriers and escorts and never carried out the part
a cavalry arm should have played in the campaigns between
New York and Philadelphia in 1777–1778. Late in 1778, Moylan
led his regiment to Connecticut, where it was scattered among
the small towns for billeting and forage and never saw action as
a unit again, although some of the officers and men served
later in the southern campaign. In February, 1780, he reported
to Washington that all except seven men of Sheldon's regiment,
also quartered in Connecticut, were unfit for duty for want of
equipment and clothing.

One cavalryman who shone through this fog of frustration
was Captain Allan McLane of Philadelphia. What aggressive
cavalry action there was in those black days at Valley Forge,
during the British occupation of Philadelphia in 1777–1778,
usually had McLane and his "Rough Riders" as a hard core.
He preyed on the British supply trains rolling into the city and
became the backbone of the American commissary department
with captured enemy food. A wealthy young man, he spent his
entire personal fortune of about £115,000 to equip and pay his
troops, and when the shortage of clothes became acute he took
his wife's household linen and had it cut into breeches for his
men and led his troopers in white linen pants, but without overcoats or boots, on many a raid in a temperature of ten above
zero. When the British officers gave a sort of Babylonian ex-
travaganza as a farewell party to General Sir William Howe in
Philadelphia, Allan McLane, probably irked by seeing as guests
the girls he had formerly danced with, led a mixed body of infantry and mounted dragoons to the doors of the festivities
where they hurled kettles filled with explosives at the British
sentries and completely broke up the party. Titian Peale's

*"Captain Allan McLane's Encounter with the British
Dragoons," by Titian Peale*

painting of McLane, cornered by six British dragoons, shows his
horse Saladin pawing at one of the British horses as the chargers
of medieval knights were trained to do. McLane killed all six
of the enemy dragoons and escaped safely and was congratu-
lated by Lafayette for this feat. As a final gesture, when the
British evacuated Philadelphia, on June 18, 1778, McLane, as
Chief Justice John Marshall described it in *The Life of George
Washington,* "with a few light horse and one hundred infantry,
entered the city, and cut off, and captured one Captain, one
Provost Marshal, one guide to the army, and thirty privates,

without losing a man." McLane was called Washington's "favorite rider" but he did not follow the army south with his commanding officer, Henry (Light Horse Harry) Lee, the father of Robert E. Lee. Allan McLane had the right idea and, on a tiny scale, sowed the seed for future irregular cavalry tactics.

A notable small cavalry unit, of only twenty-five men, and really the only one worthy of the name in 1775–1776, was the "Troop of Light Horse of the City of Philadelphia," which was founded in 1774 and is the oldest unit of its kind in the country today. Its three officers and twenty-two enlisted men were men of position and many had belonged to the Gloucester Fox Hunting Club before forming the troop. They served as mounted guards and couriers at Washington's headquarters, but this minute troop also was at the Battle of Trenton, scouted Princeton before that battle, where they captured twelve British dragoons, and covered the retreat afterwards. The troop also fought at Brandywine, Germantown, and with Lafayette at Brandy Hill. Their services were incredible in proportion to their numbers and Washington stated, "they...have shown a Spirit of Bravery which will ever do Honor to them and will ever be gratefully remembered by me."

Also there was a troop called the Marechause Light Dragoons, mostly Germans, which, under the command of Captain Bartholomew Von Heer, attended Washington as a headquarters and provost marshal guard after May, 1778, taking over the duties previously performed by various militia units and others. Other militia cavalry units came and went, and one North Carolina troop was distinguished by the fine Italian name of its captain, Casmo de Medici. South Carolina furnished two troops who received their pay and bounty in "grown" and "small" Negroes, and ·a roll in the War Department shows that 39%

11

grown Negroes were due to a Captain Barnett. Only the army could figure one out like that.

The two competing forms of enlistment, the Continental or regular army and the states' militia, plagued the army then and for years afterwards until World War I. Most men chose the militia because of more favorable enlistment terms but these troops were occasionally drafted into Continental service. For the cavalry militia, Virginia furnished the most, a corps plus one troop; and, rather curiously, Connecticut was second with five regiments, which was more than all the remaining states combined. Connecticut was the only New England state to raise any cavalry. Perhaps the state had more sporting blood than its staid neighbors, or perhaps it was because there was more open countryside to ride in.

In December, 1779, Banastre Tarleton, Oxford-educated son of a mayor of Liverpool, embarked the British cavalry in New York for the South. On the voyage most of his horses died, but he obtained new mounts by hook or crook from around Charleston, South Carolina, which was under siege by the British and which surrendered to them the next spring. Tarleton was probably the outstanding cavalry leader of the war, and because of his brilliant leadership, the British for a while threatened to sever the states south of Virginia from the others.

After Colonel Tarleton's arrival, as if by spontaneous combustion, cavalry action broke out on both sides. It was largely partisan warfare, bloody, ruthless, and cruel, waged by small marauding bands which were not part of the regular armies. On the American side, three brigadier generals of South Carolina militia stood out: Francis Marion, the "Swamp Fox," whom Henry Lee described in his *Memoirs* as "hard in visage, healthy, abstemious, and taciturn," was probably the best known;

Colonel Banastre Tarleton, by Sir Joshua Reynolds

The South Carolina cavalry leaders and
Colonel William Washington

Thomas Sumter (after whom the fort was named), younger and stronger, whom Lee called "manly and stern" but not over-scrupulous in his methods and added "enchanted with the splendor of victory, he would wade in torrents of blood to attain it"; and the third was Andrew Pickens with "a sound head, a virtuous heart, and a daring spirit."

These South Carolinians led mounted bands of rarely over a hundred white and black followers, owning their own horses and armed with rifles, who, when they approached the enemy, would dismount and leave their horses in some hidden spot in care of a few comrades. Then, victorious or vanquished, "they flew to their horses and thus improved victory or secured retreat." Their marches were long and toilsome, with men and horses seldom feeding more than once a day, and their attacks were, like the Parthians, sudden and fierce. If Tarleton had not been a foeman worthy of their steel, these new tactics would probably have harassed the British into the ocean, but he fought fire with fire and his forces of regular British cavalry and loyalist partisans generally held their own and often were victorious.

General Horatio Gates, of Saratoga fame, commanded the American forces at first and, true to the northern tradition, paid no attention to his cavalry arm despite the urgings of his cavalry commander, Lieutenant Colonel William Washington, a distant cousin of George Washington. The result was his crushing defeat at Camden in August, 1780, largely brought about by Tarleton's cavalry. A far abler general, Nathaniel Greene, succeeded Gates, and the American cavalry at last came into its own in the regular Continental Army. Greene found the local partisan bands almost as much of a hindrance as a help, for their leaders, older men than he, resented the authority of a Rhode Islander and acted as they saw fit, and he depended

*Marion's Brigade crossing the Pedee River to attack
the British under Tarleton*

largely on William Washington and Harry Lee and their small
bodies of regular cavalry.

Two of the battles in the southern theater were notable for
mounted action. At King's Mountain, in western North Carolina,
on October 6, 1780, about 1400 wild and fierce Kentuckians,
"over-mountain men," rode on horseback to a rendezvous, then,
dismounting and tying their horses with their coats and blankets
strapped to the saddles, they at once stormed up the mountain

16

where they mercilessly slaughtered the loyalists and their commander, Major Patrick Ferguson of the 71st Highlanders, the inventor of the first practical breech-loading rifle. The other engagement was at Cowpens in January, 1781, where brawling Daniel Morgan threw 150 troopers under Harry Lee on Tarleton's flank at the crucial moment of battle and turned a primary defeat into a rout of the enemy. Morgan used this small unit like a born cavalry leader and made it the neatest-fought battle of the entire war. Tarleton escaped but he suffered 830 casualties to ninety-three for the Americans. Lee's and Washington's small mounted forces gave pretty effective service under General

"Battle of Cowpens. Conflict between Colonels Washington and Tarleton." The Americans are probably in the light uniforms. Actually they wore anything available.

Greene, who wrote Lafayette in Virginia, "Enlarge your cavalry or you are inevitably ruined."

General Cornwallis advanced north in 1781 with Tarleton covering his march, and at Guilford Court House, in North Carolina, he fought with Nathaniel Greene to a standstill. The day before, Lee had gained the advantage over Tarleton in a cavalry duel but the battle was tactically a British victory although Cornwallis was so weakened that he retired to the coast, whence he advanced to Virginia in May.

After Cornwallis started north, Light Horse Harry Lee, acting with Francis Marion, attacked his line of communications and in less than two months captured five British outposts and 1100 prisoners. This achievement, combined with his previous exploits in the North, marked Lee as the outstanding American cavalryman of the war. John Marshall wrote that Lee in these operations showed the greatest fertility of invention and military resource. His son, Robert E. Lee, evidently had a running start in his military inheritance.

When Cornwallis was finally cornered at Yorktown, he had about four hundred effective cavalry under the command of Simcoe and Tarleton. Against these the Americans could pit only about a hundred dragoons, but the Duc de Lauzun commanded a crack French legion, six hundred strong, of whom a half were cavalry, and the British were effectively contained.

Two French noblemen who helped the Americans were colorful cavalry soldiers of fortune. Charles Teffin (or Tuffin) Armand, Marquis de la Rouaire, had been dismissed from the Garde du Corps in Paris for a duel over an actress and, coming to America in 1777, he had served as a colonel with Lafayette in New Jersey, had opposed the British cavalryman Simcoe, in the partisan warfare in Westchester County, New York, and had fought in Pulaski's legion in the South. In 1781 he returned to France to procure equipment for his men at his own expense which he used later at Yorktown. He was made a brigadier general by Congress in 1783. At the close of the war, Armand proposed the elimination of all the petty patrol and guard details which so dispersed the cavalry and urged the consolidation of all the units into one corps to act as a unit; in this Armand was probably right — but years ahead of his time.

The other nobleman, Armand Louis de Gontaut, Duc de Lauzun, had led a successful French expedition against the English settlements on the west coast of Africa in 1779, but, having wasted his fortune in dissipation, he came to America with Rochambeau in 1780 and commanded Lauzun's legion at the siege of Yorktown. He was an attractive fellow, this hard-fighting, amorous duke, for despite a reputation for profligacy everybody liked him for his good looks, his wit, and his bravery; and this veteran of courts, camps, and boudoirs must have brought color to the somber American army. Like Armand, he was made

Duc de Lauzun, by Jonathan Trumbull

Yale University Art School

a brigadier general, and thanked by Congress. In later years, under the title of Duc de Biron, he commanded the French Army of the Rhine against the enemies of the new republic; but as an aristocrat he was suspect. He died on the guillotine and was said to have given the traditional last glass of wine offered to the condemned to his executioner, saying, "Take it, you need courage in a trade like yours."

After Cornwallis's surrender in October, 1781, the American cavalry gradually faded away and there was no such arm in our minuscule army — which amounted to only eighty men, all told, in 1784 — until an act of Congress of March 5, 1792, authorized the formation of one company of dragoons. General ("Mad Anthony") Wayne evidently used some of these dragoons, with "The white horsehair of their brass helmets flying in the wind," to charge the Indian enemy at his victory of Fallen Timbers in Ohio in August, 1794, and their valuable services at that encounter caused Congress to increase their strength to two troops in 1796. In 1798 appeared Hoyt's *Treatise on Military Art* with the first cavalry drill regulations, according to which a regiment was divided into two squadrons of four troops each; this was certainly theory gone wild, as only two troops existed, but it probably was used by the mounted militia of the states.

In 1798, the fear of a war with France spurred Congress into increasing the dragoons to a regiment, with three more authorized, if fighting started. The uniforms were to be green coats with white facings, cocked hats bearing a black cockade centered with a tin eagle and the regimental numbers marked on white buttons. All this was mostly on paper, and in 1800, after George Washington's death, the dragoons were cut back to two troops again. By 1802 the dragoons seemed to have almost disappeared; and the whole army never had a total strength of

Published by Shelton and Kensett, Cheshire,
Connecticut, 1813. Mrs. John Nicholas Brown

*Colonel Johnson's Mounted Kentucky Riflemen charging the
British and Indians at the Battle of the Thames. The Kentuckians actually wore black hunting shirts, gray breeches, and
high-crowned slouch hats. The artist mistakenly armed these
Kentuckians with sabers. In reality they carried rifles, muskets
and possibly — some of them — long knives.*

more than 3000 for the next ten years. In 1808 a regiment of
dragoons was authorized but never raised as such, and what
dragoons there were in name served as foot soldiers.

During the War of 1812, American mounted troops only twice
played an important part, and both times it was the Kentucky
or Tennessee mounted militia, the same breed who had stormed
King's Mountain in the Revolutionary War. The first occasion
was in October, 1813, at the Battle of the Thames, near Mora-
vian Town in western Ontario, when Colonel Richard Mentor
Johnson led against the British and their Indian allies a shock
charge of mounted Kentucky riflemen which broke clean
through the enemy lines, and then, running into boggy ground,

21

dismounted and completed the victory on foot. In this fight Johnson was reputed to have killed the Indian chief Tecumseh. At the time, he was a congressman from Kentucky, and had left Washington to join General William Henry Harrison on the Canadian border. He was severely wounded in the fight and was borne from the field and became something of a national hero. In 1836 he was elected the ninth vice-president of the United States on the Democratic ticket, and during the campaign small boys chanted a popular jingle, "Rumpsey, Dumpsey, Colonel Johnson killed Tecumseh!"

The other occasion was when Andrew Jackson used his mounted Tennessee militia against the Creek Indians, who were allies of the British, in March, 1814. He attacked them in their strongholds in Alabama, first sending a force of nine hundred horsemen, under General Coffee, to destroy an outlying village. He then routed the main body of the tribe at Horseshoe Bend on the Tallapoosa River, after crossing his army over the river by mounting each foot soldier behind a cavalryman.

Congress had authorized two regiments of regular dragoons for this war but there is no evidence of their use, and in March, 1814, these two units were combined into one regiment of eight troops. In 1821, the cavalry was abolished and there was no mounted arm again until 1832, when it was revived for the Black Hawk War on the western frontier. During this blank period, the cavalry tradition was kept alive in the states' militia and it was for the use of these organizations that Lieutenant Colonel Pierce Darrow published his *Cavalry Tactics* in 1822 and 1826. The frontier had pushed westward to the Great Plains by 1832, and the hard-riding and warlike Indians of that area, who had been expert horsemen for generations, made the use of cavalry again imperative by our army.

CHAPTER II

The Old Frontier—Indians and Mexicans

1832 – 1847

ON A scorching summer's day in the year 1834, a long column of blue-jacketed dragoons rode by twos across the dusty plains of what is now western Oklahoma. At its head rode General Henry Leavenworth (after whom the famous fort had been named in 1827) and beside him, clad in buckskins and mounted on a frontier stallion, rode George Catlin, the famous painter of Indians, who had written before his departure, "I start this morning with the dragoons for the Pawnee country but God only knows where it is." Before, behind, and on the flanks of the column, a group of frolicking Comanches, the best riders of the Plains, performed feats of horsemanship which made the newly recruited dragoons goggle. When a small herd of buffaloes suddenly hove into view, the Comanches drove it, with whoops of delight, through the center of the line of march to the confusion of the troopers at that immediate spot but to the intense amusement of their comrades farther up and down the line. George Catlin quickly dismounted, whipped out his drawing tools, raised the umbrella which he carried to shade his work, and sketched the occurrence.

The origin of this regiment of reborn cavalry went back to 1828, when Representative Joseph Duncan of Illinois had intro-

*Comanches driving buffaloes through a column of dragoons.
By George Catlin.*

duced a bill into Congress to activate a regiment of "Volunteer Mounted Gunmen" (shades of latter-day Chicago!), but this bill had not passed. Then, in 1832, Congress had finally recognized the urgent necessity for cavalry on the frontier to cope with the mounted Indians of the Great Plains and had authorized a battalion of "Mounted Rangers," of six companies (the term "troop" was dropped and not revived until after the Civil War) with a total strength of 685 officers and men to serve at once in the Black Hawk War. Henry Dodge, of Michigan, was appointed major and among the six captains was Nathan Boone, a son of Daniel Boone. Three companies were sent by General Winfield Scott to Fort Gibson, near the present Muskogee, Oklahoma, on the Arkansas River, which was in the territory allotted to the Indians who had been moved or would be moved there from east of the Mississippi River.

Washington Irving in his book, *A Tour of the Prairies,* tells of a visit with these Rangers in the autumn of 1832. He described their camp as a wild bandit or Robin Hood scene, and wrote:

> In a beautiful open forest, traversed by a running stream, were booths of bark and branches, and tents of blankets, temporary shelters from the recent rain, for the rangers commonly bivouac in the open air. There were groups of rangers in every kind of uncouth garb. Venison jerked, and hung on frames, was drying over the embers in one place; in another lay carcasses recently brought in by the hunters. Our arrival was greeted with acclamation. . . . We were received in frank simple hunter's style by Captain Beane, the commander of the company, a man about forty years of age, vigorous and active. His life had been chiefly passed on the frontier, occasionally in Indian warfare, so that he was a thorough woodsman, and a first-rate hunter. He was equipped in character; in leathern hunting shirt and leggings, and a leathern forage cap.

The next year, in 1833, Congress increased this mounted body to a regiment to be called the 1st Dragoons. Dodge was promoted to colonel, with Stephen W. Kearny of New Jersey as lieutenant colonel, and Richard B. Mason of Virginia as major. All the captains of the Rangers went to the new regiment and among its lieutenants were Jefferson Davis, afterwards President of the Confederacy, and Philip St. George Cooke of Virginia, who later became the grand old man of the cavalry.

The recruiting went slowly despite the glamorous advertisements for three years' service "beyond the frontiers" and the comparatively high pay of eight dollars a month for privates. The first five companies were organized at Jefferson Barracks, just outside St. Louis, and, without uniforms, they had straggled into Fort Gibson, in mid-December, 1833, with the thermometer at eight below zero. By June, the regiment had reached only about two thirds of its authorized strength of 750 men but it was well mounted, in companies of matched horses of whites, sorrels, grays, blacks, bays, and creams, superbly equipped, and armed with a breech-loading, smooth-bore carbine of .69 caliber, the first percussion arm in the service, especially made for this regiment by Simeon North of Middletown, Connecticut.

In March, 1834, the popular writer Charles Fenno Hoffman visited Jefferson Barracks and noted in his book, *A Winter in the West,* that the dragoons remaining there were a fine-looking crowd of native Americans and well mounted, but that there were no proper facilities to train the men or horses, with consequent idleness and discontent; and all were eager to join the rest of the regiment on the frontier.

In June, 1834, with the temperature at 108 degrees in the shade, the 1st Dragoons set out from Fort Gibson as part of an ill-starred expedition under the command of General Leavenworth to make a friendly visit to the wild tribes of Comanches and Pawnees who roamed the country to the west of the established reservations where the Indians of the East had been transported and settled. This was the first of all the many mounted military expeditions into the Great Plains. Everything went wrong from the start. First, General Leavenworth was thrown from his horse during a buffalo chase and so badly hurt that he died later that summer. Then the blistering heat and the bad water, often taken from filthy buffalo wallows, and never boiled or purified, brought on an epidemic of "bilious fever" which laid low more than half the command. Colonel Henry Dodge pushed on westward with two hundred surviving dragoons, out of the original five hundred, into the Comanche country, near the headwaters of the Canadian River, where they were well received by that tribe and the Kiowas and

Pawnees, but this attitude soon evaporated in the heat of later hostilities. The Comanches for years had cruelly harassed the Mexican settlements to the south, and at first looked upon the Americans as allies against their hereditary foes. But this feeling soon changed, first to hatred against the Texans in their new republic, and then against all Americans.

The wretched remnant of the dragoons was daily weakened by the fever and finally returned to Fort Gibson with a loss by death of one third of its strength. George Catlin fell a victim and rode deliriously, alone in a nightmare, back across the prairies to Fort Gibson where he lay deathly ill, daily listening to the muffled drums of the fort's band playing "Roslin Castle" as a funeral march for the soldiers who had died.

After this disastrous good-will expedition, the regiment was used for garrison and patrol duty all up and down the line of frontier posts from Fort Snelling (St. Paul, Minnesota) to Fort Gibson in the south. Military roads were built and temporary

Smithsonian Institution

A Comanche warrior advancing, with a buffalo skin on his lance, to greet Colonel Henry Dodge. By George Catlin.

camps established. Sellers of whiskey were chased out of the Indian reservations but could not be kept away from the army posts, and one observer remarked: "Whiskey, too, is awfully abundant, and a great drawback. The soldiers will drink it; and it is most pernicious in its effects, being of the worst possible kind, and sold very cheap." The caravans going to Santa Fe were convoyed along the trail as far as the Mexican border where the incoming caravans were often picked up and escorted back to the American settlements. Then there were several long exploration trips, with meetings and councils with the Indians, such as one of 1600 miles led by Colonel Dodge in 1835 which went up the Platte and South Platte Rivers, and, turning southward, followed the Arkansas River back east, and then home to Fort Leavenworth. Other trips were made to the northwest, through what is now Iowa, Minnesota, and South Dakota, and up through Wisconsin and Illinois, and one to the Red River of the North. In 1845, Stephen Kearny, who had succeeded Dodge as colonel, led 250 dragoons again up the Oregon Trail, but this time as far as South Pass in present Wyoming, and then returned by Dodge's route of ten years before along the Arkansas River. Captain Philip St. George Cooke described Fort Laramie (now in southeastern Wyoming) with its hordes of unkempt Indians and half-breeds, as "Civilization, furnishing house and clothing; barbarism, children and fleas." A big council was held with the Sioux Indians at the fort and Colonel Kearny presented the chiefs with suitable presents and warned them of the evils of whiskey drinking. Over 3000 settlers were met moving westward along the trail, a forecast of the later grand rush which was to arouse the Indians to active hostilities.

It should be remembered that this frontier was in the territory acquired from France by the Louisiana Purchase in 1803

T. F. Rodenbough, From Everglades to Cañon with
the Second Dragoons. *Yale University Library*
Early uniforms of the Second Dragoons

and did not extend into Texas or the rest of the huge block of
land later taken from Mexico in 1848. The duty was arduous
and monotonous to an extreme, and there were many desertions,
but there were as yet no serious hostilities with the Indians;
all these expeditions had the dual purpose of exploration and of
maintaining friendly relations with the Indians.

In 1836 another mounted regiment, the 2nd Dragoons, was
authorized, primarily for immediate use against the Seminole
Indians in Florida. Colonel David E. Twiggs, a native Georgian,
known among his men as "Old Davy" or "The Bengal Tiger,"
and who they proudly boasted "cursed them right out of their
boots," became the colonel. This conflict proved the grimmest

29

and most miserable of all our Indian wars and the costliest in lives and money. It dragged on and on for about ten years, from 1832 to 1842, with the Seminoles playing hide-and-seek in the swamps and defying the frantic efforts of ten American generals, one after another, to gain a clean-cut decisive victory over their chiefs, Osceola, Wildcat, and Samuel Jones. The soldiers chanted a disillusioned jingle which seems quite applicable to the Korean impasse.

> And ever and anon we hear
> Proclaimed in cheering tones
> Our generals had — a battle? — No!
> A talk with Samuel Jones.

The 2nd Dragoons, to their natural disgust, spent most of their time, dismounted, in wading through swamps and in poling canoes through the Everglades. Their lieutenant colonel, William Selby Harney, once narrowly escaped an ambush in which the Seminoles massacred eleven sleeping dragoons; in retaliation Harney later hanged fourteen prisoners of war, for which rather drastic act he was severely criticized. The war was finally ended in 1842 by Colonel William Jenkins Worth of the 8th Infantry who defied precedent and carried on a campaign during the summer months which reached into the depths of the Everglades and destroyed the Seminole hide-outs. Years later, after the Civil War, a detachment of mounted Seminole Scouts, working out of Fort Clark, Texas, under the command of Lieutenant John Lapham Bullis, probably the greatest individual Indian fighter in the army, did yeoman service against marauding Comanches, Kickapoos, and Lipans.

The 2nd Dragoons were ordered to Arkansas and Fort Jessup, Louisiana, in the autumn of 1841, after losing six officers and

212 enlisted men, mostly from disease, during their miserable five years in Florida. At Fort Jessup two of the companies were trained as lancers, an innovation which was not lasting, for the American trooper did not take naturally to that weapon. In August, 1842, the bad news reached the regiment that Congress had passed an act dismounting it and converting it into a regiment of riflemen. This calamity was received with rage and disgust, and an unprintable song was composed highly uncomplimentary to the members of Congress; but that body soon relented and remounted the regiment in March, 1844. The consequent celebration at Fort Jessup was said to have been one for the books and included the firing of a "mounted salute" which consisted of two officers straddling the saluting cannon, one of whose trousers were set aflame by the backfire from the vent. This regiment had a tradition as "followers of Bacchus" and was considered a gay outfit in contrast to the more staid 1st Dragoons. As their song went:

T. F. Rodenbough, From Everglades to Cañon with the Second Dragoons. *Yale University Library*

The firing of the mounted salute to celebrate the remounting of the Second Dragoons in 1844

Oh! the dragoon bold! he scorns all care,
As he goes the rounds with uncropped hair;
He spends no thought on the evil star
That sent him away to the border war.

The field uniform of the dragoons during the Seminole War and the following Mexican War was a dark blue fatigue jacket trimmed with yellow (which later became the distinctive cavalry color), a flat visored cap with a wide yellow band, and light blue trousers, reinforced in the seat, with yellow stripes on the outside seams. Boots or leggings were occasionally worn. The dress uniform, which was seldom used on active service, was a short blue coat, also trimmed with yellow, and a heavy dress cap, with a long, drooping white horsehair plume attached. The officers wore an orange silk sash and the higher noncoms a yellow worsted one over their dress coats.

From 1842 until the summer of 1845, the two dragoon regiments had a spell of comparative peace and quiet, a rest from conflict which they were not to enjoy again for nearly forty years.

After Texas was admitted to the Union in the spring of 1845, war with Mexico became inevitable. Brigadier General Zachary Taylor assembled a force which included the 2nd Dragoons at Corpus Christi, Texas, during the summer and autumn of that year. Taylor, in calling on the various governors of the states for troops, asked the governor of Texas for cavalry only, as it seemed that "Texans wished to use their legs only to grasp a horse." In the spring of 1846 Taylor led his small army southward to the Rio Grande, to what is now Brownsville. The Mexicans opened hostilities by deftly ambushing and capturing Captain S. B. Thornton and sixty dragoons in late April; but

"The Brilliant Charge of Captain May at Resaca de la Palma."
The dress uniform shown is a mistake by Mr. N. Currier.

this discouraging beginning was erased by two American victories in pitched battles at Palo Alto and Resaca de la Palma on two successive days in early May.

Captain Charles A. May, son of a member of the Boston Tea Party, particularly distinguished himself at Resaca when he headed a hell-for-leather charge of eighty dragoons which tore through the Mexican lines and captured a battery of enemy guns plus a full-fledged general. Young Lieutenant James Longstreet, years later one of the Confederacy's leading generals, at this point drew his sweetheart's daguerreotype from his breast pocket, "had a glint of her charming smile" — and "with quickened spirit" sent some infantry troops to relieve May of the captured General La Vega.

The cavalry has always produced colorful personalities but May was a giant among them. He was a marvelous horseman who had previously had frequent difficulties with the law in the effete East for riding his horse up and down the steps of local hotels and for steeplechasing in the streets of Baltimore; and "with a beard extending to his breast and hair to his hip-bone, which, as he cuts through the wind on his charger, streams out in all directions, he presents a most imposing appearance." Longstreet wrote of him: "As a dragoon and soldier May was splendid. He stood six feet four without boots, wore his beard full and flowing, his dark-brown locks falling well over his shoulders." * A dragoon bold with uncropped hair, May was brevetted lieutenant colonel for his gallant conduct and will reappear later.

Taylor next moved against the city of Monterrey, the metropolis of northern Mexico. A body of mounted Texas Rangers under Ben McCulloch and Jack Hays scouted and spearheaded the march. These men in outlandish dress and with huge beards looked almost like savages and kept the Mexicans in mortal terror. They were armed with rifles and Colt's five-shooters, mounted on tough and wiry prairie mustangs, and could subsist on a daily handful of beans or corn. They were probably the best irregular horse of their times and broke up all Mexican cavalry opposition, which were usually lancers, by rifle and pistol fire. Hays's order for attack was to point at the enemy and shout, "Give 'em Hell!" He had gained a tremendous reputation as an Indian fighter in Texas and greatly added to

* *From Manassas to Appomattox* (Philadelphia, 1896).

it during the Mexican War; later he became a leading citizen of San Francisco.

General Worth, promoted for his Florida achievements, was largely responsible for the capture of Monterrey in September, 1847. Jack Hays's Texas Rangers acted as his shock troops in a wide encircling movement to the west, which isolated the city, during which the Rangers repelled one desperate charge of Mexican lancers by the superior weight of their horses and by accurate pistol fire. After that they dismounted and took a leading part in storming the outer defenses and, later, in penetrating the city by house-to-house fighting. The Rangers were credited with originating the "rebel yell" during this fighting, which afterwards chilled Yankee blood on many a Civil War battlefield. It started with a low bass rumble and rose in a crescendo to a frenzied treble shriek which suggested a sort of beserk mania of blood lust. Monterrey was a good example of the dual abilities of mounted troops. The regular dragoons, under Zachary Taylor at the other end of the city, acted largely as a reserve. The author Charles Fenno Hoffman wrote of this hard-fought battle:

> We were not many, we who stood
> Before the iron sleet that day;
> Yet many a gallant spirit would
> Give half his years if but he could
> Have been with us at Monterey.

Shortly after the Americans entered Monterrey, "Old Rough and Ready" Taylor sent Worth, in November, to occupy the city of Saltillo, about sixty-five miles to the southwest. Taylor accompanied Worth on the march, escorted by two squadrons of the 2nd Dragoons under the intrepid May.

Worth and most of the dragoons were soon withdrawn to

Nebel and Kendall, The War Between the United States
and Mexico, Illustrated. *Harvard College Library*

*The battle of Buena Vista — looking south
toward the attacking Mexicans*

join General Winfield Scott in his assault upon Mexico City by
way of Vera Cruz, and the incorrigible Santa Anna, who had
assumed command of the Mexican forces, seized this opportunity to attack Taylor and his weakened army, in February,
1847, at Buena Vista, a narrow mountain pass about six miles
south of Saltillo. Fortunately, Taylor had been reinforced in
December by a small but well-trained force under Brigadier
General John E. Wool, a native New Yorker, which included
two companies each of the 1st and 2nd Dragoons commanded

36

"Gallant Charge of the Kentucky Cavalry at Buena Vista." The Kentuckians may have worn something like these uniforms.

by the impetuous Brevet Colonel W. S. Harney who had just previously nearly lost his small command by an ill-considered raid across the Rio Grande. Also with Wool was a regiment of volunteer Arkansas cavalry under a gallant colonel with the unusual name of Archibald Yell. Wool had marched his column from San Antonio, Texas, and had captured the Mexican cities of Monclova and Parras en route without firing a shot. Besides these mounted units, Taylor also had the volunteer First Kentucky Cavalry.

Santa Anna had sent a cavalry brigade, under General Miñon, north in January, from his base in San Luis Potosí and this strong advance party had continued the Mexican tradition of drawing first blood at the expense of the American cavalry by capturing detachments of over a hundred men of the Arkansas and Kentucky cavalry regiments who were supposedly scouting Santa Anna's rumored approach but were asleep or drunk when surrounded by the Mexican lancers.

On February 20, the dauntless and long-haired Lieutenant Colonel May, with a small unit of twenty Texas Rangers under Ben McCulloch, and one squadron from each of the two dragoon regiments plus a detachment of the volunteer cavalry, sighted Santa Anna's army of about 21,000 troops coming in force toward Saltillo from the south. On the 22nd, Washington's birthday, Santa Anna attacked Taylor's small army of about 4500 men in full fury at Buena Vista, or Angostura, as the Mexicans call it. This battle raged for two days and was the bloodiest and most desperately fought engagement of the American army until the Civil War. It was a kaleidoscopic huggermugger from beginning to end. Old Zach Taylor, an inept general if ever there was one, but a superb example of courage and coolness as a man, sat calmly on his horse, Old Whitey, with one leg crooked over the pommel, in the very center of all the raging turmoil, and let his competent subordinate officers run their own shows and win the day for him. The Mexicans had about four or five thousand cavalry, mostly lancers, to the four hundred of the Americans, and they literally rode circles around the American army — but fighting and not riding wins battles and the Mexican lancers did not drive their charges home. The harassed handful of American horse did everything from escort and courier service to charging the opposing lancers, and rushed back and forth across the battlefield to plug the holes which the Mexicans kept opening. The volunteer cavalry bore the full brunt of one Mexican break-through, and Colonel Archibald Yell was killed at the head of the Arkansas regiment. The fire from a Mexican battery served by American deserters of the infamous San Patricio Battalion was particularly galling and effective. After two days of pushing and hauling and actually encircling but never dislodging the tenacious Taylor, Santa Anna withdrew his forces and retreated to the south. It was a narrow squeak and the Americans hailed it as a major victory

John Frost, Pictorial History of Mexico and the Mexican War. *Harvard College Library*

Death of Colonel Yell at Buena Vista

— which it certainly was morally; but the Americans suffered 673 casualties, of which number about 270 lie in unmarked graves on the field today.

Captain Albert Pike of the Arkansas cavalry commemorated this fabulous encounter in verse:

Ride! May to Buena Vista! for the lancers gain our rear
And we have few troops there to check their vehement career.
Arkansas and Kentucky, charge! Yell, Porter, Vaughan are slain;
But the shattered troops cling desperately unto that crimsoned
    plain,
'Til, with the lancers intermixed, pursuing and pursued,
Westward, in combat hot and close, drifts off the multitude.

CHAPTER III

Invasion and Conquest
1846 – 1848

THE CAVALRY had played a manful but always auxiliary and minor part in Zachary Taylor's early victories over the Mexicans. Then it came into its own in another theater of the war, by invading and conquering the immense areas of the Mexican territories of New Mexico and California, and by the capture of Chihuahua City, far to the south, as a sort of side show. These campaigns were all cavalry actions and, for them, the other services became, in their turn, merely auxiliaries to the mounted branch.

California and New Mexico were separated by long distances and desert country from Mexico City and connected to the United States by the commerce of the Santa Fe Trail to New Mexico and the frequent calls of whaling and trading ships to the California ports. The conquest of this huge area was the primary objective of the war. So, immediately after the outbreak of fighting, Colonel Stephen Kearny of the 1st Dragoons assembled a force at Fort Leavenworth to strike at Santa Fe and then to push on to California.

This force was named "The Army of the West" and was composed of some three hundred men of the 1st Dragoons, the 1st Regiment of Missouri Mounted Volunteers under Colonel Alexander W. Doniphan, and a St. Louis mounted body of about a hundred men called the Laclede Rangers. Attached to these

41

General Kearny's dragoons leaving Las Vegas, New Mexico, on their march to Santa Fe

mounted troops were a battalion of artillery and two small companies of volunteer infantry.

On June 5, 1846, this small army got under way, leaving Fort Leavenworth in detachments, at intervals, with orders for the whole force to reassemble at Bent's Fort on the Arkansas River near the present Las Animas, Colorado. These units followed the well-beaten Santa Fe Trail and arrived without untoward incidents at the rendezvous in late July and early August. From there, Kearny led his troops up over the steep Raton Pass and down into New Mexico. Village after village surrendered as he moved on southward toward Santa Fe, then an adobe town of some 3500 souls. The Mexican governor made an initial pretense of making a stand at the impregnable Apache Canyon, about twenty-eight miles east of the town, but his unwilling troops melted away as the Americans approached; and on

R. G. *Gibson*, Journal of a Soldier under Kearny
and Doniphan. *Harvard College Library*

General Stephen Watts Kearny

August 18, Kearny's cavalry rode into Santa Fe, where he issued a proclamation declaring New Mexico to be a part of the United States and its inhabitants American citizens.

Behind Kearny came two other bodies of reinforcements: another volunteer mounted force of 1000 men under Sterling Price, a member of the Missouri legislature, and an infantry battalion of Mormons recruited from a large number who had been recently driven from Nauvoo, Illinois, and had gathered at Council Bluffs, Iowa, with the plan of going to California. As soon as these troops arrived in Santa Fe in September, Kearny left Price in command there, and soon afterwards placed the Mormon Battalion under the command of Captain Philip St. George Cooke of the 1st Dragoons, with orders to follow close behind. Kearny rode on toward California, at the head of three hundred regular dragoons.

Captain Cooke wrote in his diary:

> Tomorrow, three hundred wilderness-worn dragoons, in shabby and patched clothing, who have been on short allowance of food, set forth to conquer or annex a Pacific empire, to take a leap in the dark of a thousand miles of wild plains and mountains, only known in vague reports as unwatered, and with several deserts of two or three marches where a camel might starve, if not perish of thirst. Our success — we never doubt it, and the very desperation of any alternative must insure it.

Brigadier General Kearny, for he had received word of his promotion, led his troopers south down the Rio Grande valley where he soon ran head-on into the famous frontiersman Kit Carson who was spurring his way toward Washington, D. C. He carried dispatches from Commodore Robert F. Stockton, U. S. N., and Lieutenant Colonel John C. Frémont, the "Pathfinder," announcing the surrender of California by the Mexicans to a combined force of sailors from Stockton's squadron and of members of Frémont's expedition which had been nominally exploring the Far West. Carson had been a guide with Frémont and had been picked to ride to Washington with the glorious news and had been making record time and exhausting mules on this dangerous dash through Apache land. Carson's home was in Taos, New Mexico, and a stop to see his recent bride had priority on his schedule.

The news, however, was premature and had been sent impulsively, for the Mexicans soon afterwards rebelled against the handful of occupying Americans but to Kearny, a stern and rigid officer, it was a bitter disappointment to have his thunder stolen by a naval officer and by the histrionic Frémont, whom he looked upon as a grandstander performing under the wing of his politically powerful father-in-law, Senator Thomas Hart Benton of Missouri. Frémont, incidentally, had just been appointed lieutenant colonel of the newly formed Mounted Riflemen, a regiment which we shall meet later, but which he never joined.

Kearny then sent back to Santa Fe all the wagons in his train and two hundred of his men and, packing his supplies on mule back and practically kidnapping the highly reluctant Kit Carson as a guide, he set out on a dash for the Coast with one hundred picked dragoons, mostly mounted on mules, and two twelve-pounder howitzers which became the bane of the expedition but were the first wheeled vehicles to cross what is now the state of Arizona. Carson's dispatches were turned over to a substitute rider and the flying column headed due west from the Rio Grande, up into the main chain of the Rockies.

Headed by Kit Carson, the dragoons rode up and up, past the

old Santa Rita copper mines, to the headwaters of the Gila River which they followed on its westward course to its confluence with the Colorado River, where Yuma, Arizona, now stands. They hit the river at a point about 4300 feet above sea level where it flowed clear and swift from the wooded mountains with a width of about fifty feet and an average depth of two feet. This was beautiful land with excellent grazing for their mounts, deep in the heart of Apache country, but a force of one hundred well-armed dragoons was immune from the attack which would surely have fallen upon a small body. The Apaches even came in to trade, and the dragoon camp was once enlivened by a plump, middle-aged squaw who galloped about completely naked, a sort of Rocky Mountain maenad, hellin' and squallin', until she completed a dicker for a dragoon's red flannel shirt. The scenery was gorgeous but the going was tough, for the way often pinched down in a canyon to the boulder-strewn bed of the river and poor Lieutenant Davidson, in charge of the two wheeled howitzers, seldom made camp until late at night, and often did not arrive until the next day. Time and again the harassed lieutenant was forced to take his howitzers apart, pack them on his mules, and reassemble them when the going made it possible to use wheels; an object lesson obviously unknown to a motor-mad member of our General Staff who was recently reported to have naively stated that "a jeep can go anywhere a horse or mule can." The march was vividly described by Lieutenant W. H. Emory in his *Notes of a Military Reconnaissance,* the official report sent to Washington, which was later published by the government.

The expedition finally broke out of the mountains onto the flat desert, a relief to the harassed Davidson but a hardship to the horses and mules, for the good grazing disappeared;

passing north of Tucson, it reached the junction of the Gila with the Colorado River in late November. There dispatches captured from enemy couriers told of the uprising of the Mexicans in California against the forces of Stockton and Frémont, and Kearny rode on by forced marches over the Sierras until he arrived at Warner's Ranch near San Diego. A little beyond, at San Pasqual, he ran into a sizable force of Mexican lancers. The dragoons, mostly mounted on mules, rashly charged the enemy, which nearly proved the end of Kearny and his dragoons, for they ran into a neatly prepared ambush in which a third of his force was killed or wounded. Incidentally, the howitzers were not used. If the Mexicans had possessed the tactical abilities of the Comanches there would have been no American survivors. Kearny's small force was then extricated by the arrival of reinforcements from the American naval squadron at San Diego, and all safely reached the haven of that port, thus completing the first trip to the Pacific Coast by troops of the United States Army.

Behind Kearny, leaving Santa Fe in October, 1847, came the Mormon Battalion of about 340 men under the command of Captain Philip St. George Cooke, of the 1st Dragoons, a Virginian and West Pointer, who later remained loyal during the Civil War and became a major general in the Union Army. His daughter, however, married J. E. B. Stuart, the famous Confederate cavalry leader, and there were stresses and strains in the family. With Cooke was young Lieutenant George Stoneman, who later became a Union general and, after the Civil War, a governor of California. The Mormon Battalion was really an infantry column with a wagon train and it took a route considerably south of the Gila River to get through. It was the first expedition to reach the coast with wagons south of the Oregon

Trail. This was the only practical southern route for wagons and later for a railroad, but somehow it was overlooked in the peace treaty with Mexico in 1848, so that it became necessary for the United States to acquire this area by the Gadsden Purchase of 1853. On the way, Cooke's battalion captured Tucson, Arizona, without firing a shot, and the only conflict it had was an extraordinary battle with a large herd of wild bulls which attacked the column and disemboweled many horses and mules and wounded several men. Cooke's command finally reached California in January, 1847, too late to take a part in any fighting.

Harper's Weekly, June 12, 1858.
Harvard College Library

Lieutenant-Colonel Philip St. George Cooke, in command of the Mormon Battalion

Marching with the Army of the
West. *Harvard College Library*

Alexander William Doniphan

While Kearny was dashing for California, Colonel Alexander
William Doniphan and his regiment of Missouri Mounted Volunteers had conducted a lightning campaign of seven weeks to
put down the Navajo Indians, west of Santa Fe, and in December, 1846, they were poised on the Rio Grande, near the hamlet
of Socorro, for a march on Chihuahua, far to the south.

Doniphan and his command were unique. A tall, red-headed,
frontier lawyer, he knew nothing and cared less about military
science. Later, during the Civil War, he once stood back-to-back
with Abraham Lincoln to compare their heights and overtopped

49

"D—mn a mule, any how."

John T. Hughes, Doniphan's Expedition.
Harvard College Library

*"D—mn a mule, any how." One of Doniphan's men
having difficulties with his mount*

the President by half an inch, which caused Lincoln (who had
not read modern whisky advertisements) to remark that he was
the only man of distinction he had ever met that "came up to
the advertisement." His men were country boys with a marked
aversion to discipline, but natural riders and marksmen, full of
fight and vinegar, and used to frontier hardships.

With this force, and an accompanying wagon train of traders
who wanted to get their goods to Chihuahua, Doniphan conducted a campaign which is a dream to those allergic to army
red tape. He broke every rule in the game — and was completely successful. During the year of their enlistment, these
volunteers, starting at Fort Leavenworth, covered 3600 miles
by land and 2000 by water to return to Missouri. They had no
quartermaster, no paymaster, no commissary, no uniforms, no
tents, and no discipline. They rode south into Mexico, handily
defeating superior enemy forces in two pitched battles by sheer
exuberance and reckless courage, and captured El Paso and
Chihuahua. They raised complete hell in both places, and then

One of Doniphan's men who shocked General Wood

J. D. Tisdell.   CROSVENOR

THE VOLUNTEER.

went on to join forces with General Wool in Saltillo in May, 1847. Wool reviewed them upon their arrival, some dressed like Mexicans and some like Comanches, and that rigid martinet must have shuddered in his boots. Their one-year enlistments had expired by that time, and from Saltillo they rode to the mouth of the Rio Grande and embarked for New Orleans and home. It was a brilliant march with great facets of humor and a complete joy to those iconoclasts who believe that fighting, and not frills or paperwork, is the main object of an army.

Doniphan was an honest man. His speech at a welcome-home banquet to himself and his men was described as follows:

> He gave the boys a great deal of credit. . . . In describing the battle of Brazita said he "I remained behind on the hill overlooking the battle as any prudent commander would. I soon found the Mexicans were overshooting the boys who were below me. Their shot were falling thick all around me. I put spurs to my horse, charged to the front, hallowed 'Come on boys.'" Said he "The boys thought I was brave as h-ll, but they did not know what drove me there." *

While Kearny's and Doniphan's cavalry were overrunning New Mexico and California, the commanding general of the army, Winfield Scott, had collected a force, partly taken from the protesting Taylor, which landed near the great Mexican port of Vera Cruz, on the Gulf of Mexico, in early March, 1847, and captured that city by the end of the month. In April, Scott started up the old Spanish National Highway, leading into the mountains and interior, with the capital, Mexico City, as his objective. The cavalry reverted to a minor role in this invasion of the enemy's heartland, and Scott at first only had three companies of the 1st Dragoons, six companies of the 2nd Dragoons, and the newly raised regiment of Mounted Riflemen which had lost nearly all of its horses on the sea voyage and whose men mostly had to serve on foot — than which no greater humiliation could be inflicted upon a cavalryman.

The Mounted Rifles, with distinctive green trimmings on their blue jackets, had been authorized by an act of Congress in May, 1846, for the specific purpose of guarding the Oregon Trail, but this mission had been tacitly waived for the time being and the regiment joined Taylor's army in October. Its

* Joseph H. McGee, *Story of the Grand River Country* (Gallatin, Missouri, 1909).

senior officers had originally been political appointees and were notoriously incompetent, with the notable exception of its first colonel, Persifor F. Smith, a Princeton graduate and Louisiana lawyer, who was "a simple, scholarly, unassuming man, but all ranks appreciated his ability, attainments, clear perception, valor, promptness and steadiness." Smith had served with distinction in the Seminole War and with Taylor in the northern

New York Historical Society

"U.S. Dragoons Cutting Their Way through a Mexican Ambuscade," by N. Currier. Mr. Currier is wrong again in showing the regulars in dress uniforms while campaigning.

Mexican campaign where he was made a brigadier general. He was succeeded as colonel by an outstanding cavalryman, Edwin Vose Sumner, a regular army officer from Boston, which was a rare bird indeed in those days, whom Dabney Maury of Virginia, a lieutenant in the regiment, fresh out of West Point, described as "a rough old dragoon." Under Sumner, the regiment would go out to drill with its full complement of officers but return under the command of brevet second lieutenants, the political officers having been relieved by Sumner for inefficiency. A surgeon of the regiment said, "The officers were all gentlemen, brave and generous to a fault — but the most cantankerous lot I ever met."

Two of the regiment's younger men in Mexico later gained distinction; Second Lieutenant Dabney Maury, who became a major general in the Confederate Army and wrote well of his experiences in *Recollections of a Virginian,* and Sergeant (later Major) William B. Lane, whose wife's book on cavalry life on the frontier, *I Married a Soldier,* is a classic of the Old Army.

The real Beau Sabreur of Scott's army, however, was Captain Philip Kearny of Newark, New Jersey, a nephew of General Stephen Kearny, who had been born with the proverbial silver spoon in his mouth. A graduate of Columbia College, he had been commissioned a second lieutenant in the 1st Dragoons in 1837 and had been sent to France to study cavalry tactics at Saumur; while there he had found a way to serve with the *Chasseurs d'Afrique* in the fighting in Algeria. He later resigned his commission but rejoined the dragoons at the outbreak of the Mexican War and commanded General Scott's personal mounted bodyguard from Vera Cruz to Mexico City. His men were mounted on dapple-gray horses which he had selected and paid for himself; and Mayne Reid, the famous writer of boys' books, who served in Mexico, wrote that this squadron rode by with "the hoofs of all striking sumultaneously — as if they were galloping to set music." Phil Kearny lost an arm at Mexico City and resigned from the army in 1851. He then went back to France and served on the French staff, in Italy in 1859, at Magenta and Solferino, in which battles he took part in every cavalry charge and won the Cross of the Legion of Honor. In the Civil War he became a major general of the New Jersey Volunteer Cavalry, but was killed in 1862 at Chantilly; after the battle, Robert E. Lee, who had known him in Mexico, sent back his body to his wife, together with his sword, horse, and saddle.

Soon after starting up the highway to Mexico City, Scott met Santa Anna's army — reorganized since its setback against Zachary Taylor at Buena Vista — at Cerro Gordo, a seemingly impregnable position in the mountains blocking the road to the capital. Because of a brilliant and hazardous reconnaissance made by Captain Robert E. Lee, Scott was able to outflank, smash through, and rout the Mexican army — and the way to Mexico City lay wide open. During this battle, the Mounted Rifles, serving unhappily on foot, suffered eighty-four casualties.

Soon after this victory, the Rifles managed to mount two companies, who then served with the dragoons, but the majority of the regiment slogged on up the highway with the rest of the infantry. The two mounted companies found their long-barreled rifles a clumsy weapon to use on horseback, in contrast to the short cavalry carbine, and would fire one shot and charge the enemy rather than go through the contortions of reloading while mounted.

Scott finally reached the outskirts of Mexico City in August, 1847, and again defeated the Mexicans on two successive days at Contreras and Churubusco. During the latter battle some of the Mounted Riflemen, serving on foot, captured some Mexican horses and, quickly mounting, charged into the melee. Captain Philip Kearny led his picked dapple grays in a hell-for-leather charge which went way beyond the American lines. The recall was blown but Kearny did not hear it in the excitement of the battle, and while most of his followers pulled up, he, standing upright in his stirrups, actually charged with about a dozen men into one of the city's gates to capture a battery of guns. "Oh, what a glorious sight it was to see Phil Kearny riding into them!" wrote an enthusiastic soldier. The little group jumped from their horses to capture the guns — and saw they were alone. The confusion of the enemy momentarily saved them and, quickly remounting, they charged back through the retreating Mexicans, but a stray shot shattered Kearny's arm. General Winfield Scott, years later, called him "the bravest man I ever knew and a perfect soldier."

During the famous storming of Chapultepec Castle, just before the American entry into Mexico City, the Mounted Riflemen charged the heights on foot and Lieutenant Morris had the somewhat unusual experience of leading a faltering detachment of United States Marines who had lost their officers. When the American army marched into the city, the next day, the flag of the Mounted Rifles was raised over the National Palace and General Scott, escorted by Kearny's dragoons, and in all the superb carriage of his six feet four inches, doffed his hat to the Riflemen drawn up before the palace and, bowing low, said "Brave Rifles! Veterans! You have been baptized in fire and blood and have come out steel." These words were taken as the regimental motto and have been kept by the successor organization, the 3rd Cavalry, to the present day.

Nebel and Kendall, War Between the United States and
Mexico, Illustrated. *Harvard College Library*

General Scott's entry into Mexico City with dragoon escort.
These were the uniforms worn during the war by the regulars.

The Americans occupied Mexico City for nearly nine months,
until the end of May, 1848, when a treaty of peace was finally
ratified. During this time, Mexican guerrillas constantly
harassed the long American line of supply which stretched from
Mexico City, through Puebla, up and down towering mountains, to the fever-ridden seaport of Vera Cruz. To combat these
guerrillas, Colonel Jack Hays, of Monterrey fame, brought another regiment of mounted Texas Rangers to Mexico City and
these, in conjunction with the regular dragoons, waged a war

A Texas Ranger

to the death against these Mexican irregulars. The Texans put
the absolute fear of God and Texas into the Mexicans, as was
their tradition, and shot to kill at the slightest affront. When one
Ranger officer was assassinated while riding through a tough
district of Mexico City, there were more than 80 bullet-riddled
Mexican corpses found in that section on a morning shortly
afterwards. General Joseph Lane, who had been one of Zachary
Taylor's chief officers at Buena Vista, commanded this anti-
guerrilla unit, and a part of it was formed by men of the 3rd
Dragoons, a regiment recruited for the duration of the war only,
among whose officers was Major William Polk, a brother of
President James K. Polk and a former minister to Naples. Other
detachments of this transitory regiment served under Sumner

and Harney, the commanding officers of the Mounted Rifles and the 2nd Dragoons.

After the ratification of the peace treaty of Guadalupe Hidalgo, the Americans evacuated Mexico City in May, 1848, and the last troops embarked at Vera Cruz in July. The cavalry, while small in numbers, had guarded well the long, vital highway to Mexico City and had practically eliminated the threatening activities of the mounted Mexican guerrillas against this life line of the American forces.

CHAPTER IV

The New Frontier, New Enemies, and New Regiments

1848 – 1861

By the terms of the peace of Guadalupe Hidalgo, Mexico lost about one half her area, and the United States, if Texas is included, gained about one third of its present-day size. This was a huge area — all dynamite — which, except for the American settlements in East Texas and the Mexican hamlets around the Rio Grande valley in New Mexico and along the coast of California, was inhabited almost entirely by wild animals, principally enormous herds of buffaloes, and by roving and savage tribes of mounted Indians who based their economy and ways of life on the wandering buffalo herds. West of the 100th meridian and to the coastal Sierras, the average rainfall was not enough for agriculture, and before the day of irrigation, deep artesian wells, and dry farming it was quite generally believed that this would remain Indian country for years to come. But protection had to be given to the established settlements and to the westward-creeping frontier, which were under constant Indian attack, and also to travelers on the Oregon Trail to the fertile Northwest, on the old Santa Fe Trail, and further south on the San Antonio-El Paso road. The great Mormon migrations to Utah, beginning in 1846, and the horde of gold-seekers rushing to California, starting in 1849, worried and angered the no-

Mounted Navajo warriors, by H. B. Möllhausen.
They seem discouraged.

madic Indians who sensed the end of their rights in this vast area.

The United States Army had only three cavalry regiments to cover this enormous territory, which had increased the interior lines to be protected against hostile Indians from about 2000 to 12,000 miles and the number of warlike Indians some fivefold. Besides these responsibilities, the United States had agreed to prevent the Indians, which meant especially the Apaches and Comanches, from using this former Mexican territory as a base for raids into the Republic of Mexico. The Indians could not understand this for they depended on their raids into Mexico to supply their meat and quite logically said, "We must steal from somebody; and if you will not permit us to rob the Mexicans, we must steal from you or fight you." This was spreading the cavalry woefully thin, and to allow it as much freedom as possible several chains of forts were established in the threatened areas in which the housekeeping was usually done by infantry detachments with the cavalry used as a mobile force which could ride out to protect or punish. This was still inadequate but it took Congress seven years, until 1855, to realize it.

Texas was the most vulnerable spot and suffered the most. The Indians, particularly the dreaded Comanches who had developed a high skill in mounted warfare, soon learned the trick of retreating to Mexico after a raid into Texas and vice versa. Also Mexican bandits and American renegades took advantage of the protection of international law and raided back and forth across the border. From the west the Apaches added their numbers to the Comanche threat, and both used the unmapped region of the Staked Plains as a base of operations for forays that sometimes drove through the Texas settlements as far as the Gulf of Mexico. From the north, the young braves on the established reservations, in what is now Oklahoma, would become bored and restless and to break the monotony of good behavior would sneak away and raid the settlements to the south and retreat to the sanctuary of their reservations when pursued. Texas got it from the three sides and became the main theater of our cavalry operations. One chain of forts was established in that state along the Rio Grande to guard the border, and another on a north-and-south line just west of Austin and San Antonio to ward off the raids from that direction; although often enough in the 1850's the Indians slipped through these cordons and penetrated far behind them.

To show how thinly our cavalry was spread, at the end of the year 1848, the 1st Dragoons had three companies in the Territory of New Mexico (which then included the present state of Arizona), three more in California, and one each at Fort Leavenworth, at Fort Scott which was about a hundred miles south of Fort Leavenworth (both were on what is now the easterly boundary of Kansas), and at Fort Washita which was still further to the south in present-day Oklahoma; and one company was far to the north on the Mississippi River above Fort Snelling (St. Paul, Minnesota). The 2nd Dragoons also had its ten companies scattered, with six in Texas and two in New Mexico; and two were on their way overland to California.

The 3rd Dragoons, which had been authorized for the duration of the Mexican War only, had been completely disbanded; and the Mounted Riflemen were having all kinds of discharge and enlistment troubles at Jefferson Barracks, Missouri, because some guardhouse lawyer had discovered a technicality which necessitated the discharge of all the enlisted men and the recruitment of the entire regiment anew. The Rifles had orders to fulfill their original mission, the guarding of the Oregon Trail, as soon as their ranks were refilled.

In May, 1849, the Mounted Riflemen, having recruited their strength, rode out westward by detachments to establish a chain of posts along the Oregon Trail. In command was Lieutenant Colonel William W. Loring of Florida, whose father, Reuben L. Loring, had moved south from Hingham, Massachusetts. The colonel had lost an arm at Chapultepec but this was considered a minor disability among the iron cavalrymen of that time and he went on to an extraordinary military career. Along with most of the top brass of the cavalry he later threw in his lot with the Confederacy and rose to be a major general in its army. After the Civil War, he led a group of Confederate officers to Egypt, to enter the service of the Khedive, where he remained for ten years. He took part in the Abyssinian campaign of 1875–1876 and rose to be a general of division and was made a pasha with all the highest decorations of the Egyptian government. Loring probably rose highest of all the throng of unreconstructed Rebels who flocked abroad, after the Civil War, to rebuild their fortunes in foreign lands. He finally returned to the United States, as did most of the others, and wrote a highly interesting book about his experiences, *A Confederate Soldier in Egypt.*

William Wing Loring as an Egyptian pasha

W. W. Loring, A Confederate
Soldier in Egypt.
Harvard College Library

The Mounted Rifles made good time along the Oregon Trail, following it up the Platte River, branching off up the North Platte River, then up the Sweetwater River, across the Continental Divide through South Pass, and to Fort Hall on the headwaters of the Snake River, in what is now southeastern Idaho. Along the way, detachments were dropped off to establish posts at Fort Kearny (named after General Stephen Kearny, who had died the year before) on the Platte River near what is now Grand Island, Nebraska, and, 350 miles further west, at Fort Laramie on the upper reaches of the North Platte River in present-day eastern Wyoming. Another post had been planned at Fort Hall but this was not established because of the scarcity of forage in the neighborhood. From Fort Hall, Loring led his remaining men on to the Columbia River and down that to the Willamette Valley.

The Rifles found the Oregon Trail jam packed with gold-seekers rushing to California and encountered many comic and tragic reliefs, often helping stranded groups who had rushed off to the promised land in ill-prepared impetuosity. They had no trouble with the Indians, who had not yet been goaded into hostility and seemed more curious than antagonistic, but they had difficulty in grazing their horses and mules because the tidal wave of "forty-niners" had used up most of the grass along the trail. Accompanying the troops were George Gibbs, a naturalist and graduate of Harvard College, and an artist, William H. Tappan of Boston, who — unfortunately for this book — sketched more of the scenery than of the incidents of camp life or the doings of the Rifles.

After the arrival of the Rifles in Oregon, they melted away by desertions like snow on a summer's day. The pay of the privates was eight dollars a month, and the wages in the California gold camps ran as high as thirty dollars a day; and many of the men had probably enlisted anyway as a means of securing safe transportation to the Coast. Once about a hundred men deserted in a body but the capable Colonel Loring pursued and brought back seventy of these. By 1851 the regiment had been so depleted by desertions that it was returned to Jefferson Barracks where it was again recruited and then sent to Texas where its nominal colonel, Brevet Brigadier General Persifor F. Smith, was in command of the Department of Texas. The Indians in Oregon and along the Oregon Trail were still comparatively peaceful and the services of the Rifles were badly needed in Texas where the Indians were lacerating the frontier.

The companies of the 1st and 2nd Dragoons which had been sent overland to California had left Monterrey, Mexico, in July, 1848, and had traveled by way of Parras and Chihuahua to hit Philip St. George Cooke's westward route along the Gila River, and from there over the Sierras to the Coast. Colonel Richard B. Mason of the 1st Dragoons became military governor of California, and among his worries in that turbulent time and place was the same rash of desertions among the dragoons which plagued the Rifles. In 1851 Mason died and was succeeded by Lieutenant Colonel Thomas Turner Fauntleroy of Virginia, who resigned in 1861 to become a brigadier general in the Confederate Army. (What resonant names some of those mid-nineteenth-century American officers had — Steptoe, Archibald Yell, Bodfish, Gideon Pillow, David Twiggs, and Fauntleroy!)

Hardly had the fighting ceased in Mexico when the inimitable and long-haired Lieutenant Colonel Robert May of the 2nd Dragoons, who had made such a name for himself, received a crushing blow where it hurt the most; for General Order No. 25 from Washington of July, 1848, read:

> The hair to be short, or what is generally termed "cropped." The whiskers not to extend below the lower tip of the ear and a line thence with the curve of the mouth. Moustaches will not be worn (except by cavalry regiments) by officers or men on any pretense whatever.

This underhanded attack on the cavalier tradition must have upset the ebullient colonel, but not for long; for a bit later, while commanding at Fort Mason, Texas, on the Llano River, he established himself as a sort of second Messiah among the Indians. The post surgeon had received some chloroform, whose anesthetic qualities had just been discovered, and Colonel May secured a bottle for his own purposes. At his next meeting with some of the Indian chiefs, May loftily announced that he had been recently endowed with the divine gift of restoring life to the dead and that he would be glad to show his powers if one of his visitors would be kind enough to volunteer for the demonstration. Not an Indian moved.

"Well," said Colonel May, "I am depressed by your obvious lack of confidence in my abilities, but perhaps that small dog at your heels may do to prove my powers, and, with your permission, I shall retire and put him to death."

The debonair colonel reappeared shortly with the seemingly lifeless body of the dog which he placed upon the ground. "Now," he announced, "I am going to present you all with a souvenir of this momentous occasion," and he proceeded to slice off a piece of the dog's tail for each chief. The dog did not move and the Indians were convinced of its demise. May then announced that he would restore life to the corpse and carried the dog to a tent, from which it emerged shortly afterwards barking and frisking about. The Indians were awe-struck and ever afterwards, when on the war path, carefully avoided Colonel May. The pieces of the dog's tail were considered big medicine and cherished in each brave's medicine bag for years afterwards.

It might be well at this point to dispel a rather popular illusion about the "noble red man" which seems to have stemmed from the romantic novels of James Fenimore Cooper. No matter what the Indian of the East may have been, and there is strong reason to believe that Cooper was talking through his hat, the Indians of the Great Plains were savage, cruel, and filthy beyond words. True, they were shamefully treated upon numerous occasions but, on the whole, every effort was made, especially by the army, to convince them of the futility of resistance and to settle and civilize them on the reservations. But it usually didn't take, and the atrocities which the Indians committed on the frontier settlers, especially on the women, are almost unbelievable and completely unprintable. When an officer was unable to accompany his wife on a dangerous trip through hostile Indian country, he invariably ordered a trusted subordinate of the military escort to fatally shoot her if capture by the Indians became inevitable. The feeling was so intense in Texas that General Persifor F. Smith, a mild and cultured man, ordered that "All predatory Indians . . . will be pursued, attacked, and put to death," and "It is not deemed advisable to take prisoners."

The Comanches became so troublesome in Texas in 1850 that three companies of Texas Rangers were sent to help the 2nd Dragoons, who were desperately trying to cover a huge territory with a handful of men. This tribe was probably the most dangerous of all. They were expert horsemen, usually well armed, carrying thick rawhide shields which could actually deflect bullets, and had developed such a high degree of skill in mounted tactics that they were called "the finest light cavalry the world has ever seen." Their bailiwick was in the unmapped reaches of the Staked Plains of West Texas, a region which was unknown to the Americans until well after the Civil War. From this retreat they would pour out on furious raids, usually during the full of the moon, against the American and Mexican settlements, and would leave a swath of terror and destruction be-

Harper's Weekly, May 1, 1858.
Harvard College Library

An Indian Foray in the West

hind them, killing the men, stealing the livestock, and bringing back as prisoners the younger women and some children to be brought up in the tribe.

Most people, when they think of the frontier Indian fighting days, visualize Custer's last stand against the Sioux and Cheyennes in what is now Montana. But the northern Indians, with certain notable exceptions, did not become actively hostile until the outbreak of the Civil War; whereas the fighting against the Apaches, Navajos, Lipans, Kiowas, Kickapoos, and Comanches in the Southwest was continual from the annexation of Texas in 1845 until well into the 1880's. It was so continual that it would be impossible to describe the innumerable cavalry skirmishes with the Indians in a book of this kind.

A few yearly examples will show what the cavalry was up against during the 1850's.

In October, 1853, Captain John Williams Gunnison and a detachment of Mounted Rifles, who were making a survey for a railway route from the Mississippi River to the Pacific Ocean, were all killed by Indians near Sevier Lake, Utah.

Young Captain Michael Van Buren of the Mounted Rifles, who had gallantly served in the Mexican War, was pierced through the stomach by an Indian arrow during an encounter near San Diego, Texas, in July, 1854. No surgeon was available and his men guarded him from further attack until medical help arrived two days later, when the arrow, which protruded through his back, was removed; but the wounded captain died within the week.

In January, 1855, a detachment of 1st Dragoons, under Lieutenant Samuel D. Sturgis, chased a war party of Indians from Galisteo, New Mexico, for 160 miles in two days, and killed three and wounded four, with a loss of one dragoon killed and

T. F. Rodenbough, From Everglades to Cañon with the Second Dragoons. *Yale University Library*

"Dragoons" before and after becoming "cavalry"

two wounded. It was so cold that the men's hands became too numb to reload their carbines during the encounter and they were forced to fight with their sabers. During the same month Captain Stanton and several men of this regiment were killed in a fight with Mescalero Apaches on the Peñasco River in southeastern New Mexico.

In November, 1856, Second Lieutenant Horace Randal of the 1st Dragoons and twenty men chased a band of fifty Apache horse thieves over three hundred miles through the snow-covered mountains of New Mexico, making eighty miles on one

71

day's ride, attacked the Indians, and recovered all the stolen horses.

In April, 1857, Second Lieutenant Walter Jenifer of the 2nd Cavalry (a new regiment which we will meet shortly), at the head of thirteen men, chased a war party of a hundred Indians in Texas over three hundred miles for thirteen days. An advance party of the lieutenant and seven men on foot, in rocky country, were attacked by the Indians whom they repulsed and safely regained their horses.

There was not always an officer available for emergencies and, in 1857, Sergeant Charles Patrick and twelve men of the 2nd Cavalry chased a larger band of hostiles in Texas for seven days, covering 160 miles in the last three days, caught up with the Indians, and inflicted heavy punishment upon them.

These are just random examples of what went on all the time during the small cavalry patrols led by junior officers or non-coms during this decade.

An uncommon young officer, Second Lieutenant Jerome Napoleon Bonaparte, just out of Harvard and West Point, reported for duty with the Mounted Rifles in Texas in July, 1852. His grandfather, Jerome Bonaparte, had married Miss Elizabeth Patterson of Baltimore but had returned to Europe, at his brother Napoleon's insistence, to become the king of Westphalia. The grandson served with credit on the Texas frontier for two years and then resigned to enter the French army under his imperial cousin, Napoleon III. He served in Italy, Algeria, and the Crimea, and had risen to a lieutenant colonelcy at the outbreak of the Franco-Prussian War in 1870. After his cousin's surrender, he escorted the Empress Eugénie to England and then returned to the United States, where he died in 1893.

72

The New Frontier, New Enemies, and New Regiments

In March, 1855, a new day for the cavalry dawned when Congress authorized two new mounted regiments — almost a miracle — but to confuse things these were named the 1st and 2nd Cavalry Regiments. Later, shortly after the outbreak of the Civil War, all the mounted regiments were given the name "cavalry" and numbered by seniority, but that is added confusion which we shall meet later. It was about time for these

National Archives

Lieutenant Jerome Napoleon Bonaparte of the Mounted Rifles, in Texas, 1852

Lieutenant-Colonel Robert E. Lee
of the Second Cavalry

reinforcements, for the harassed dragoons and mounted riflemen had been run ragged for seven years trying to cover all this
new territory without any addition to their numbers.

Jefferson Davis was the Secretary of War under President
Franklin Pierce at the time and was afterwards accused by his
enemies of packing these new regiments with his favorite
officers who later went with the Confederacy. This probably
was untrue, although the majority of the field officers of all the
mounted regiments were southerners or became southern sympathizers during their service. Anyway, the first colonel of the

1st Cavalry was the Bostonian Edwin Vose Sumner, the two majors were John Sedgwick of Cornwall, Connecticut, and William H. Emory of Virginia, who had written a report of General Kearny's march to the Pacific and later acted as "astronomer" in running the boundary line with Mexico after the peace in 1848 and again in 1853 for the Gadsden Purchase. George B. McClellan of Pennsylvania, later commander of the Army of the Potomac, was a captain. All of these officers remained loyal. But the lieutenant colonel was Joseph E. Johnston, and J. E. B. Stuart was a captain, and both of these Virginians rose high in the Confederate Army.

With the 2nd Cavalry, which was called "Jeff Davis's Own," it was a more one-sided story. The colonel was Albert Sidney Johnston of Texas, the lieutenant colonel was Robert E. Lee of Virginia, Earl Van Dorn of Mississippi was a brevet major, Edmund Kirby Smith of Florida (his father came from Litchfield, Connecticut) was a captain, Theodore O'Hara of Kentucky, who wrote "The Bivouac of the Dead," was a lieutenant, as were Charles E. Travis of Texas, son of William B. Travis, the hero of the Alamo, John B. Hood of Kentucky, and Fitzhugh Lee of Virginia, a nephew of Robert E. Lee. All of these officers, except Travis, won fame in the Confederate Army.

The only officers of the regiment who became prominent in the Union Army were Major George H. Thomas of Virginia (the Rock of Chickamauga) and Captain George Stoneman of New York, who had been with the Mormon Battalion and who later became Chief of the Cavalry Bureau and a governor of California after the Civil War.

The 1st Cavalry was organized at Fort Leavenworth and the 2nd at Jefferson Barracks; after they were equipped and trained, the 1st was ordered to the nearby Fort Riley, which later became the leading cavalry post of the country and the site of the Cavalry School. The 1st had its real initiation to Indian fighting two years later at a battle with the Cheyennes on the Solomon River. The 2nd, however, was sent to Texas to relieve the Mounted Riflemen, and the regiment rode through Arkansas and Indian Territory in full strength on its splendid horses which had mostly been bought in Kentucky and were the finest obtainable. It was the best mounted regiment the country had ever seen, with each company riding horses matched in color, and indeed it was a thrilling sight to see "Jeff Davis's Own" ride by behind Albert Sidney Johnston and Robert E. Lee.

The three different names for the mounted regiments were quite perplexing. All the five mounted regiments were light cavalry; the heavy cavalry of the European armies, such as the cuirassiers, with their steel breastplates and helmets and their heavy horses, who depended on shock action with the saber, the *"arme blanche,"* never existed in the United States Army. These regiments differed a little in their uniforms and arms. They all wore the regular short blue jackets, the dragoons with orange trimming, which color had superseded yellow for them in 1851, the riflemen with green, and the cavalry with yellow. The dragoons and rifles "exulted in the Albert Hat," as Colonel Albert Brackett expressed it in his book *A History of the United States Cavalry,* which was published in 1865, and the hats bore orange or green pompons to match their jacket trimmings. The new "cavalry" regiments, however, got a sort of cloak-and-dagger black slouch hat which Brackett compared to one worn by "Fra Diavolo" and called it "an ungainly piece of furniture." The brim of this was pinned up on the right side by a metal American eagle, and on the left side black ostrich feathers sloped bushily backwards: three for field officers, two for com-

Uniforms of the Army of the United States
1774–1889. *Harvard College Library*

*Uniforms of cavalry and dragoons, 1855–1858, showing what
Albert Brackett called the "Albert cap" of the dragoons, and the
"Fra Diabolo" hat — "an ungainly piece of furniture" — of the
cavalry. By H. A. Ogden.*

pany officers, and one for enlisted men. Brackett snorted that the enlisted men delighted in contorting their bedraggled feathers into ludicrous shapes and that this new headgear was much inferior to the old dragoon cap which had been graceful and soldierly.

The arms of the mounted regiments differed too. The dragoons carried carbines, also called musketoons, suspended on a sling belt over the right shoulder when riding, and Prussian-type sabers and horse-pistols. The riflemen carried percussion-lock rifles and Colt's army revolvers but no sabers. The cavalry had sabers, percussion rifled-carbines of .58 caliber, but for some mysterious reason were given Colt's navy revolvers. Incidentally, the Colt repeating revolver revolutionized Indian fighting, for its long barrel gave it range and its repeating capacity broke up the old Indian tactic of drawing fire and then charging before there was time to reload. The saber was generally considered a useless nuisance in Indian fighting and was often discarded in the field.

During the years 1855–1856, Captain George B. McClellan of the 1st Cavalry was a member of a commission of American officers which toured Europe and visited the scene of the Crimean War. From this trip Captain McClellan brought back the saddle used by the Prussians formed on a Hungarian tree, and this model, with certain modifications, was adopted by the United States Army for its mounted troops. The "McClellan Saddle" remained standard equipment until the horse cavalry was abolished in 1942.

Besides the continual brushes with the Indians which the small detachments on patrol and reconnaissance had, there were also plenty of larger engagements with comparatively heavy losses on both sides. In fact there were twenty-two distinct Indian wars during the decade of the 1850's. The following were among the more notable of these clashes.

In 1852, Lieutenant Colonel Edwin V. Sumner, the Boston dragoon, led a punitive expedition against the Navajos, who had been raiding the upper Rio Grande settlements in New Mexico. The chase led into the famous Canyon de Chelly, now a national monument in northeastern Arizona, where the Indians stopped the dragoons in their tracks by rolling down huge rocks from the steep walls of the canyon. Although the losses were not heavy on either side it was a definite repulse to the column and meant many a further skirmish before the Navajos were brought under control. During this expedition, the song was composed which was sung to "stable call" by the bugle.

> Come get to the stable, as fast as you're able,
> Water your horses and give 'em some corn,
> For if you don't do it, the colonel will know it
> And then you will rue it, as sure's you're born.

Two years later, in March, 1854, a war party of 250 Utes and Jicarilla Apaches attacked a detachment of sixty dragoons, about sixteen miles south of Taos, New Mexico, which was led by Lieutenant John W. Davidson, of the 1st Dragoons, the same long-suffering officer who had sweated the two howitzers to California in Kearny's march in 1846. In this fight his command was overwhelmed, and only Davidson, the surgeon, and seventeen men escaped alive after a fight of three hours, and most of the survivors, including the two officers, were badly wounded. It would seem that Davidson was a child of misfortune, but he afterwards rose to be a brevet major general of United States Volunteers during the Civil War, and was another Virginian who fought in the Union Army.

To avenge this defeat, Lieutenant Colonel Philip St. George Cooke of the 2nd Dragoons pursued the victorious Indians with two hundred men and succeeded in killing six Indians and dispersing the band. Kit Carson, by then happily domesticated in Taos, left his hearth and wife to guide this punitive column. Carson for a short time had served as a lieutenant of the Mounted Riflemen after his ride to the coast with General Kearny in 1846.

The next month, far to the north on the Platte River, in what is now Nebraska, a band of Brulé Sioux massacred Lieutenant John L. Grattan and twenty-nine men of the 6th Infantry. This was not a cavalry action, except on the part of the Indians, but the old dragoon, General William S. Harney, headed a punitive column, composed of horse and foot, which set out the next year, in 1855, and caught this tribe on Blue Water Creek, a tributary flowing into the North Platte River from the north. Our old friend Lieutenant Colonel Philip St. George Cooke was along and led a cavalry charge into the Sioux camp which resulted in a complete rout of the Indians, who had eighty-six killed, five wounded, and seventy women and children captured, while the troops only suffered twelve casualties. The scalps of two white women were found in the Indian camp. In this action Lieutenant John Buford of the 2nd Dragoons particularly distinguished himself and this officer later made his mark as a leader of Union cavalry in 1861–1865.

Further west, in April, 1855, in what is now Colorado, Colonel Fauntleroy of the 1st Dragoons fought a pitched battle with a large war party of the Utes, a tribe which gave much trouble, on the Arkansas River, about twenty miles from Poncha Pass (near Salida, Colorado), and killed forty Indians and wounded many others. Three days later, Fauntleroy defeated them again, and for a while, the Utes returned to their reservation and remained quiet.

In 1856, the Mounted Riflemen moved west from Texas to New Mexico, leaving the new 2nd Cavalry, which had ridden cross-country from Missouri, to guard Texas, a man's-size assignment if ever there was one. That same year, the 1st Dragoons established their headquarters at Fort Tejon, California, between Bakersfield and Los Angeles, in Kern County, but the regiment was scattered all over the West Coast and in Arizona and New Mexico. The 2nd Dragoons were centered around Fort Riley and the new 1st Cavalry around Fort Leavenworth, and both these regiments became active in preserving order in Kansas Territory.

The next year, 1857, saw the usual amount of frontier engagements, with two outstanding. Lieutenant John B. Hood (later the famous commander of the Texas Brigade in the Confederate Army) left Fort Mason, Texas, in July with a scouting party of the 2nd Cavalry and orders to attack any Indians off their reservations. He met a war party, was wounded himself, and six of his men were killed or wounded, a victory for the Indians.

That same month, Colonel Sumner, at the head of six companies of the 1st Cavalry, fought with three hundred well-mounted and armed Cheyennes, a most formidable tribe, on the Solomon River in present-day Kansas, and drove them off the field by a charge.

Among the Americans wounded in this fight with the Cheyennes was Lieutenant J. E. B. Stuart. Years afterwards, Major General D. S. Stanley, who had served in the Union Army, recalled this near-escape of the later Beau Sabreur of the Confederate Army in his *Personal Memoirs:*

I rode after a party of Indians who seemed to keep together. Occasionally they turned in their saddles and fired at us without checking their ponies. J. E. B. Stuart rode on my left. Our horses were greatly used up as this breakneck speed had been kept up for four miles. Suddenly a big, fat Indian slid off his horse and fired at Stuart. I turned my horse and rode in on the Indian, firing one shot, but as I fired near my horse's ear, it scared him, and immediately jumping off my horse, I tried to get a good aim at the Indian, when to my horror my pistol stood firmly cocked and refused to fire. The Indian saw my fix in a flash and ran towards me, presenting his pistol. I threw my pistol to the ground, drawing my sabre and turned around my horse's head to avoid the Indian's shot, and at that moment Stuart dashed his horse upon the Indian, cut him on the head with his sabre and laid him prostrate. But in the same instant, the cool old chief put the bullet he had intended for me into Stuart's breast. The Indian was killed and for a time we thought Stuart was mortally wounded.

But Stuart recovered to meet death later from another dismounted enemy, a Union cavalry sergeant of General Custer's Michigan Cavalry, whose horse had been shot from under him and who killed the dashing Confederate leader with a random pot shot.

In 1857, the conflict in "Bleeding Kansas" between the slavery and free state factions reached a climax, and a detachment of the 1st Cavalry was brought in under Lieutenant Colonel Joseph E. Johnston to maintain order. This unit, through Johnston's tact and firmness, had no trouble with either faction although the bullets whizzed all around it. It was a ticklish situation. Colonel Sumner's sympathies must have been with the free state faction, and his lieutenant colonel's directly the opposite, and it speaks well for the moderation of both officers that they were able to maintain a neutral attitude.

*Colonel Sumner with two hundred dragoons ordering
a crowd of eight hundred to disperse before the
legislative hall in Topeka in 1856*

Later that year, the largest body of troops ever assembled on
the western frontier was sent, under the command of Colonel
Albert Sidney Johnston of the 2nd Cavalry, to escort certain
government civil officers to Salt Lake City. The Mormons had
flouted all federal authority since their initial emigration to
Utah in 1846 and it was felt that these officials should be backed
with a show of strength. This force spent the winter near
Fort Bridger, in what is now the southwestern corner of Wyoming, and suffered terribly from the cold and lack of forage for

the animals, for the Mormons had followed a scorched-earth policy and destroyed the grazing. The 2nd Dragoons, under Lieutenant Colonel Philip St. George Cooke, lost a third of their mounts during this miserable winter of 1857–1858. In the spring, the army entered Salt Lake City, which had been evacuated by the Mormons, and found that beautiful place like a city of the dead, so quiet was it as the army marched through its deserted streets. There was no fighting and Colonel Johnston soon reached a reasonable understanding with Brigham Young and the Mormon elders which restored a normal way of life; and the troops were gradually withdrawn.

During that same spring of 1858, there was a severe engagement by three companies of the 1st Dragoons, in Oregon Territory, in which the Indians killed several dragoons, but a punitive force caught the hostiles near the junction of the Snake and Tucannon Rivers, in what is now southeastern Washington, and the dragoons won a bloody revenge by a charge with sabers through the mounted enemy. The Indians put on a superb display before this battle, with the finery of their gorgeous plumes, war bonnets, and wild trappings, with bead and feather fringes fluttering from their bridles, and eagle feathers and plumes stuck in their horses' manes and tails.

> By heavens! it was a glorious sight to see
> The gay array of their wild chivalry.

Back in Texas that autumn, Brevet Major Earl Van Dorn and four companies of the 2nd Cavalry rode ninety miles in thirty-eight hours for a surprise attack on a Comanche village, into which they made a headlong charge and won a complete victory. No quarter was given, and about eighty braves were killed. Van Dorn followed this up with another attack in which he, Fitzhugh Lee, and E. Kirby Smith were wounded and several men killed. These two engagements were the most decisive victories gained to that time over these dreaded Ishmaels of the Southwest.

From 1856 on the great experiment with camels began in Texas and other parts of the Southwest. These animals were brought from Tripoli and Syria, by direction of Secretary of War Jefferson Davis, to see if they could supplement the horse in the arid desert country, and there was even talk of forming a camel corps in the army. The camels did not work out too well; they scared the living daylight out of the horses, and the American troopers had had no experience in the care or hand-

Harvard College Library

"Embarkation of the Camels at Smyrna, 1856"

ling of these cantankerous beasts; but before they could be given a fair trial, the Civil War began and the camels were turned loose on the desert, where for years afterwards they frightened the lonely prospector and cattleman. The Apaches, who would eat anything that moved, from snakes on up, were believed to have finally ended this interesting experiment.

During the small remaining time before the outbreak of the Civil War, the conditions along the Rio Grande became almost anarchic. General David Twiggs had stripped the border garrisons of troops to fight the Indians, and Mexican bandits at once proceeded to ravage the Texas setttlements. One especially notorious and bold, Juan Nepomuceno Cortinas, even captured and sacked the town of Brownsville in the autumn of 1859. Twiggs went on leave in 1860, and Lieutenant Colonel Robert E. Lee of the 2nd Cavalry took over the border command and at once went to the Rio Grande valley and arranged a working agreement with the Mexican authorities to curb the border lawlessness, but left two companies of his regiment there to lend weight to the understanding.

In December, 1860, South Carolina seceded and the great struggle began. In January, 1861, a Texas convention voted to secede. The federal troops were scattered throughout the state and General Twiggs, a native Georgian, who had reassumed command, surrendered all federal posts and properties to Ben McCulloch's Texas troops, the same McCulloch who had commanded a body of mounted Texas Rangers in the Mexican War. Most of the officers of the 2nd Cavalry joined the Confederacy when Major Earl Van Dorn returned with a batch of signed commissions after a quick visit to President Jefferson Davis of the Confederate States at Montgomery, Alabama, then the Confederate capital. Robert E. Lee did not join this initial rush and returned to Washington before following Virginia out of the Union, in April, 1861.

The few officers of the 2nd Cavalry who remained loyal eventually made their way to the Gulf coast and managed to obtain transportation for themselves, and what men they had salvaged from the wreckage, to New York, whence they went to Carlisle Barracks, Pennsylvania, to recruit the regiment in the North.

The other regiments were mostly stationed outside the authority of the Confederacy and so were not surrendered en masse, but there were many resignations by the officers and a few desertions among the enlisted men to join the Confederate forces. A few northern officers who had become southern sympathizers by association met the problem by resigning and remaining neutral during the war. The ineffable Colonel Robert May was one of these. He resigned his commission and became a vice-president of the Eighth Avenue Elevated Rail Road in New York City — a far cry indeed from the battlefields of Mexico and the plains of Texas for the miracle man of the Indians.

CHAPTER V

The Confederate Cavalry
1861 – 1865

THE SOUTHERN STATES had certain advantages in the cavalry arm over the North at the beginning of the Civil War. Most of the experienced officers of the mounted service, including four full colonels of the five regiments, were southerners and resigned their commissions in the United States Army as their individual home states seceded from the Union; they usually obtained commissions of a higher grade in the Confederate Army or with the volunteer regiments of the different southern states. But most of these officers, such as Robert E. Lee, Albert Sidney Johnston, Richard S. Ewell, Joseph E. Johnston, Thomas T. Fauntleroy, Earl Van Dorn, Dabney Maury, William Wing Loring, E. Kirby Smith, Joseph Wheeler, John B. Hood, and others, soon became general officers. As such, they assumed wider responsibilities and naturally could not act as pure cavalrymen, although they made good use of their former practical experience in handling the mounted arm. Besides the valuable services of seasoned officers, the South could draw on a population to whom riding and hunting had been second nature all their lives, and the consequence was that the Confederate cavalry started off with a rush and held a pronounced lead during the first part of the war.

Neither side at first knew quite how to use its cavalry in the farming country of the East where the first major engagement took place, at Bull Run, on July 21, 1861. The officers who had been accustomed to Indian fighting tactics on the Great Plains were a bit taken aback by the comparatively immense numbers of the armies in the field and had a tendency to follow the cavalry tactics used by the European armies of the time which placed stress on the shock charge with the saber. However, the natural American genius for invention and adaption eventually changed these ways, so completely inappropriate to the American terrain and temperament, to a system whereby the mounted troops fought mounted or afoot, almost always with firearms, and used their horses mainly for speed and mobility of movement. These methods completely revolutionized cavalry strategy and tactics and were later adopted by the more progressive European armies. So successful were they that the cavalry played a part in the American Civil War which was comparable to its importance in the Middle Ages — or, possibly, a better comparison would be with the Napoleonic wars.

An English cavalry officer of the Napoleonic wars once said that the purpose of cavalry in warfare was to give tone to what otherwise would be simply a vulgar brawl. If ever a man gave tone to a war, it was James Ewell Brown Stuart, Major General "Jeb" Stuart, C. S. A., commanding the Cavalry Corps of the Army of Northern Virginia. A graduate of West Point in 1854, he had served with the Mounted Rifles and then for six years with the 1st Cavalry in Kansas, where he had been wounded in Sumner's fight with the Cheyennes on the Solomon River in 1857. Before that, young Stuart had courted, and wed, at Fort Riley, Kansas, in 1855, Flora Cooke, the daughter of Colonel Philip St. George Cooke of the 2nd Dragoons, the old Indian fighter from Virginia who had commanded the Mormon Battalion on its march to the coast and who remained loyal to the

Union. The Cooke family was split asunder by the Civil War, for another daughter married the Surgeon General of the Confederate Army, still another a Union general, and the son, John R. Cooke, a Harvard graduate, became a brigadier of North Carolina Infantry and was not reconciled to his father for twenty years.

Jeb Stuart was the last of the cavaliers and filled the eye. In his twenty-eighth year, he was nearly six feet tall, with a flaring, bronze, spade beard and long mustachios, and a thorough dandy in his dress. He wore a flowing gray cloak lined with scarlet, white buckskin gauntlets, and carried a light saber belted over a yellow silk sash with tasseled ends. On his short gray jacket he would wear a red rose in season, and a lovers'-knot of red ribbon when the roses were not in bloom. His wide-brimmed slouch hat was held up on the right side by a gold star, and a white ostrich feather curled back on the left. He was an elegant man and as able as conspicuous. Gay and social, he loved singing and music and even had his own personal banjo player, one Joseph Sweeny, ride constantly by his side to play on the march or at an impromptu dance at the night's stop. But if it was Saturday night the party shut down promptly at midnight, for Jeb Stuart was a devoutly religious man and, for all his gaiety and high spirits, a complete teetotaler to boot.

The final song at a party, accompanied by Sweeny's thumping banjo, always was the crashing chorus, with the girls joining in:

> If you want to smell hell —
> If you want to have fun —
> If you want to catch the devil —
> Jine the Cavalry!

"Gen. J. E. B. Stuart's Ride around McClellan, June 1862."
The artist, H. A. Ogden, did not draw Stuart's hat
and ostrich feather correctly.

Stuart was a humorist as well for, besides a banjo player, he carried along a telegraph operator on his slashing raids behind the Union lines and it was his custom to tap the enemy wires, and, after gleaning as much useful information as the time allowed, he would have his man send out a bevy of confusing orders, or as he did once, wire the Quartermaster General of the Union Army, to complain of the bad quality of the Federal mules which seriously handicapped the moving of captured wagons.

Twice Jeb Stuart, leading his cavalry of the Army of Northern Virginia, raided completely around the opposing Union armies. The first time was when General McClellan was practically on the doorstep of Richmond, Virginia, in June, 1862, and Stuart with 2500 cavalry destroyed communications, burnt millions of dollars' worth of property, captured hundreds of prisoners, horses, and mules, and gave the supercautious McClellan and his army an extreme case of the jitters. (Incidentally Stuart and McClellan had served together in the old 1st Cavalry on the Kansas plains before the war.) From the information gathered on this circuit dash, Lee confidently sent Stonewall Jackson to fall on McClellan's rear and flank in the Seven Days' Battle, with the result that the panicky powers in Washington ordered McClellan to evacuate his army by water. The Richmond newspapers rejoiced in the thought that Jeb Stuart had outwitted his father-in-law, Philip St. George Cooke, who commanded McClellan's cavalry.

Later that same year, in August, Stuart again rode behind the Union lines and attacked the rear of General Pope's army, inflicting large damage and capturing Pope's personal baggage and his private and official correspondence. From this information, Lee again sent Stonewall Jackson on a turning movement of the Federal lines which resulted in the complete defeat of Pope at the Second Bull Run, or Second Manassas, as the Confederates called it.

Jeb Stuart's other complete circuit of the Union Army, and his greatest raid, was into Pennsylvania the following October, when he led a cavalry force of 1800 men with four pieces of light artillery to capture the towns of Mercersburg and Chambersburg in the rear of the whole Federal army and ninety miles from the Confederate lines. He moved clockwise, coming up from the west, and making a wide sweep to the east to return, after inflicting great damage. The Federal cavalry frantically galloped around in circles trying to intercept Stuart, and Alfred Pleasonton, leading some four hundred cavalry, ran into the raiders on their return as they approached a ford on the Potomac River. Stuart immediately attacked mounted, charged the enemy off the crest of a hill, dismounted, and held the hill while his column safely crossed the ford below, after bluffing a Pennsylvania regiment of infantry, which was guarding the ford, into withdrawing by an audacious demand for its surrender. He had ridden ninety miles in the previous thirty-six hours but his pursuers were even more exhausted and there was no pursuit across the river into Virginia. His loss was one wounded and two missing — and two of his fine personal mounts, which his servant, Mulatto Bob, lost, with himself, by trying to sustain the march on Pennsylvania applejack. It was a risky and rather unfruitful raid but its audacity and brilliance of execution were what made Jeb Stuart's name a byword.

By the next June, in 1863, Major General Stuart commanded a cavalry corps of 12,000 men and twenty-four pieces of artillery and the Confederate cavalry was at its peak. In the first week of that month a grand review of the entire corps was held on the plains near Brandy Station, Virginia, which was a gala affair to which the cream of the Confederacy were invited. In a way it was like the ball of the Duchess of Richmond on the eve of Waterloo, for four days later the largest cavalry battle of the war was fought on almost the same ground. The Confederate dignitaries, the governors of several states, and the loveliest women of the South watched the most colorful and inspiring sight in all military pageantry as the great bodies of Stuart's horsemen passed in review; first at a walk, then at a trot, and

Pictorial Battles of the Civil War.
Harvard College Library

General Fitzhugh Lee leads a charge of Stuart's cavalry at Kelly's Ford, Virginia, on the Rappahannock River, March 17, 1863

finally at a thunderous gallop with pennons and flags waving, to the crashing accompaniment of artillery salutes and the stirring music of martial bands. It was the spiritual high-water mark of the Confederacy.

On June 9, Stuart led this force against 15,000 Federal cavalry at the battle of Brandy Station, which was a swirling huggermugger of an affair, with fighting mounted and afoot along a three-mile front, and drove the enemy back across the Rappahanock River. This was the largest cavalry engagement of the war and probably marked the combat zenith of the Confederate mounted service. After that, and the Battle of Gettysburg the following month, the superior resources of the North and the hard schooling the Union cavalry had received at the hands of Stuart and other southern cavalrymen began to pay off in increased strength and efficiency, whereas the Confederates slid off by attrition and lack of supplies, especially in suitable remounts, for the Confederate trooper was required to supply his own horse — a regulation which caused much trouble and lost time after the fine first mounts of 1861 were used up.

Jeb Stuart's part at Gettysburg has been the subject for much debate. Before the battle, he went off on an independent raid in which he captured 125 supply wagons and 1000 prisoners (which slowed him down considerably), whipped Kilpatrick, the Union cavalryman, captured Carlisle, Pennsylvania, burnt the United States Cavalry Barracks there, and immobilized 15,000 Union troops in that region: all with only eighty-nine casualties. But he left General Lee in the dark as to his movements and Lee badly missed his reconnaissance reports, whereas his foe was well served in that respect. On the third day of the battle, Stuart, who had rejoined Lee, attempted to gain the rear of the Union lines but was repulsed by the vigilant squadrons of

Buford, Gregg, and young Custer. The Union cavalry was coming into its own at last.

Jeb Stuart was killed at the age of thirty-one, at Yellow Tavern Virginia, in May, 1864, at the head of about 1100 cavalry, opposing a dash for Richmond by General Phil Sheridan and 8000 Union troopers. He was caught in a melee with Custer's Michigan Cavalry and shot down by a dismounted sergeant in blue. Stuart was probably the most dashing cavalry officer of the war, and Robert E. Lee's words about him serve as a proud epitaph: "General Stuart was my ideal of a soldier"; and, what possibly meant even more to a cavalryman, "He never sent me a false piece of information."

Another outstanding Confederate leader of horse arose in the West, Nathan Bedford Forrest of Tennessee, who enlisted as a private at the age of forty and rose to be a lieutenant general in the Army of Tennessee. Forrest was a complete amateur in warfare and perhaps it was his freedom from rote and tradition and his frontiersman's craft and cunning which allowed him to develop some most original and effective cavalry tactics. The Confederate general Dabney H. Maury (once with the Mounted Rifles) said he "was born a soldier as men are born poets," and some consider him the greatest cavalryman of the war. He was a strong, lithe, fine-featured man over six feet tall, but almost completely unschooled, who had made a small fortune in livestock and slaves before the war. Forrest has been labeled uncouth because his speech was in the dialect and his spelling irregular, and he said himself, "I never see a pen but what I think of a snake." But his written comment across a private's third application for a furlough was clear enough to the luckless trooper: "I told you twicest Goddamit know." In reality, he was a man of dignity and poise except when angered, when his

Lieutenant-General Nathan Bedford Forrest

whole personality changed and he became terrible to behold.
He seems to be best known for his advice on how to win battles,
which has undoubtedly been twisted by time and humorists into
an extreme hillbilly rendering: "Git thar fustest with the most-
est" — which, regardless of how it was said, makes plenty of
sense, and especially so as Forrest usually carried it out.

Forrest was an original and cut his cloth for the occasion. Once he engaged a nine-gun Union ironclad on the Cumberland River with his troopers and drove it off down the river by their accuracy of fire through the portholes — about the only instance in history of cavalry fighting the navy, and defeating it. Another time, he actually captured several Union gunboats on the Tennessee River and manned them for a while with his cavalrymen. He was bold and effective, mounted or dismounted, and his men did everything the situation demanded, from acting as engineers and sailors on gunboats to serving in the line of battle as infantry. Once, when he was wounded and unable to ride a horse — and he was wounded several times and had twenty-nine horses shot from under him — he led his men in a horse and buggy, with his shattered foot painfully propped up over the dashboard.

The exploits of this amateur in warfare were fabulous. He commanded the Confederate cavalry at Fort Donelson in February, 1862, and cut his way through the Union lines before the rest of the garrison surrendered. After Shiloh he guarded the retreat with only 350 men and charged three enemy regiments with shotguns and put them to rout, although he was badly wounded in the action. In July, 1862, he began his slashing raids against the Federal lines of communications and with 1000 ill-equipped troopers he captured General Crittenden and 1765 men, and huge quantities of supplies, at Murfreesboro, Tennessee, from which he armed his followers. Twice again that same year he repeated this sort of raid, both times capturing immense supplies from superior forces.

Probably his greatest feat was his relentless pursuit of Colonel Streight's raiding cavalry column into Alabama in May, 1863, when he pursued a force of 1700 men with but 500 followers,

*General Forrest leaving one of the twenty-nine
horses shot from under him*

riding on an average of forty-one miles for three days, with a
final spurt of ninety miles in the last forty-eight hours, charging
and pressing the invaders constantly, and then by sheer bluff
forcing the superior enemy to surrender to supposedly greater
numbers, while his completely worn-out men nodded sound
asleep in their saddles. In the conference before the surrender,
Forrest had his small detachment of horse artillery ride along a
road behind him, which Streight could see, and then turn back,
out of sight, onto the road again so that it seemed as if a continuous stream of artillery was passing. Streight counted the

same guns five times and surrendered. According to Dabney Maury, Forrest described Streight's reaction, when he learned he had surrendered about 1700 men to 400 remaining pursuers, as follows:

> "I told him 'Stack your arms right along there, Colonel, and march your men away down into that hollow.'
>
> "When this was done," continued Forrest, "I ordered my men to come forward and take possession of the arms. When Straight [sic] saw they were barely four hundred, he did rare! demanded to have his arms back and that we should fight it out. I just laughed at him and patted him on the shoulder, and said, 'Ah Colonel, all is fair in love and war, you know.'"

There was never a man like Forrest. Since the days of Richard Coeur de Lion there has seldom appeared a man who so fired the enthusiasm of men by his primitive lust for personal combat combined with brilliant leadership and planning. Men sought eagerly to serve under him, even deserting from other units to follow him. Almost always he gave them victory over great odds. It was only the personal enmity of Braxton Bragg, first as his superior commander and then as personal adviser to President Jefferson Davis, which prevented Forrest's advancement to greater fields. Grant described him as "about the ablest cavalry general in the south," and Lee said that perhaps the ablest cavalry commander of the Confederacy was a man he had never seen — Forrest.

With one of his favorite mounts, a large twelve-year old gray gelding named "King Philip," it was a case of like master, like horse. Sluggish on ordinary occasions, King Philip became superbly excited in battle and, laying back his ears and throwing up his tail, he would leap forward across the field to snap his teeth at anything in a blue uniform. After the war, King

Philip's spirit, like those of many other good Confederates, seemed to have been broken. He even allowed himself to be used in harness. One day, while drawing an old lady down the street in a buggy, he suddenly noticed a group of policemen in blue uniforms. Up went his tail, back his ears, and with teeth bared he charged down the street with the buggy bounding behind him. Women screamed and the policemen ran for their lives. Philip then slowed down to a despondent amble and with a long sigh became again the docile hack.

This natural military genius, Forrest, was made a lieutenant general in the twilight of the Confederacy, in February, 1865, and was finally overwhelmed by General James H. Wilson, whom we shall soon meet, on the latter's great raid to Selma, Alabama, in which Wilson adopted many of the tactics originated by his opponent.

Another amateur cavalry leader, who rose high in the western theater of war, was John Hunt Morgan of Kentucky who gained the name of the Rebel Raider. Morgan was to the manner born and a leading citizen of Lexington, who had served with the Kentucky cavalry at Buena Vista in the Mexican War. He became a colonel and began his startling raids in 1862 and showed an ingenuity which compared with Forrest's. His men depended completely upon their firearms for weapons and had an utter contempt for a cavalry shock charge with sabers. When the Union cavalry resorted to the *arme blanche* and came galloping headlong with drawn sabers at Morgan's riflemen who had dismounted to receive the brunt, their comment was "Look at those fools again with sabers! Give it to 'em!" And a blasting wave of fire easily repelled the charge. When, in their turn, Morgan's men charged, they often fired double-barreled shotguns at close range, and clubbed their way through with their gun butts.

General John Hunt Morgan — the Rebel Raider

This was all contrary to the tenets of European cavalry experts but it worked well in America and Morgan's claim as the originator of these mounted infantry tactics may be as good as any.

His forces never reached 4000 and yet he killed and wounded nearly as many of the enemy and captured 15,000 more. He was called the author of the far-reaching raid into enemy country in contrast to the cavalry dash behind the opposing lines, and, up to a certain point, he performed miracles in capturing needed arms and supplies. He also used the technique of tapping the Union telegraph wires to gain information and to send confusing orders over a false signature. And he carried on a feud with a Louisville newspaper editor to whom he sent insulting telegrams from his raids, and who, in turn, wrote derogatory editorials, calling Morgan a horse thief, which were eventually read with rage by the Rebel Raider.

His raids in 1862 were brilliantly executed and were made into Kentucky from Tennessee. Acting rapidly, and avoiding fighting when possible, Morgan would thrust hard at his objective and then, splitting his command, he would strike right and left to confound his enemies, and reunite later at a rendezvous. His original purpose in raiding Kentucky, besides the capture of desperately needed supplies, was to obtain recruits, for he and his family were well known and influential in that state, and he issued a poetic recruiting proclamation in Lebanon, Kentucky, which read

> Strike for the Green Graves of your Sires!
> Strike for your Altars, and your Fires!
> God and your Native Land!

and went on to call for 50,000 Kentuckians to rise and join the Confederacy.

Alas, for all the hopes the Confederacy pinned on Kentucky, the state furnished more soldiers to the North than to the South.

But Morgan's early raids were wonderful. On one, in July, 1862, he set out with 900 men from Tennessee and returned with 1200. He had traveled 1000 miles, captured seventeen towns (in which he destroyed all government arms and supplies), dispersed 1500 home guards, and captured and paroled 1200 Union troops — and all this with but ninety casualties to his own force. His men carried only their arms and one hundred rounds of ammunition and lived completely off the country, picking up fresh mounts as needed, which was why he was called a horse thief by the editor in Louisville and by others in the North.

The morale and pride of his troopers were at their peak during that golden year of the Confederacy and his men exulted in their successes. One Texas regiment which was in his command for a while broke into song (possibly over the change in scenery and climate):

> The morning star is paling; the camp fires flicker low,
> Our steeds are madly neighing, for the bugle bids us go,
> To put the foot in stirrup and shake the bridle free
> For today the Texas Rangers will cross the Tennessee.

As the war progressed, his men deteriorated in type and habits, and toward the end they did considerable looting of private property, especially in goods from stores and money from banks.

In June, 1863, John H. Morgan went on his greatest raid, which ended in failure, far to the north on the Ohio-Pennsylvania boundary. General Braxton Bragg had ordered him to raid into Kentucky to break the Union communications between Nashville and Louisville, but Morgan, who did not get on with the cautious Bragg, disobeyed orders and crossed the Ohio River into Indiana, whence he turned east into Ohio, passing through the suburbs of Cincinnati, and pushed on, through snowballing opposition, to the Ohio River, at a point opposite West Virginia. Floods had made the river impassable and only a few, Morgan among them, were able to reach the opposite shore. Upon seeing the plight of those left behind, Morgan returned to the Ohio side, and led a small band, who escaped the encompassing Union forces, on northeastward, until he was forced to surrender near the Pennsylvania line. July, 1863, was a bad month for the Confederacy, with the surrender of Vicksburg, and the repulse at Gettysburg, as well.

This drawing of Thomas Nast's for Harper's Weekly *was an extreme example of war propaganda. A close inspection will show the Confederate Raiders, presumably Morgan's, committing or about to commit every outrage on the calendar on this pitiful town — most of which, at least as shown, was untrue.*

Morgan and his officers were shamefully treated as common convicts by their captors and confined in the Ohio State Penitentiary at Columbus. One of the most humiliating punishments to the younger officers was the required shaving of their heads and beards, upon which latter adornment much time and effort had been lavished. About four months after their incarceration, Morgan and several of his officers escaped by tunneling out of their cells and safely reached the Confederate lines.

Upon his return, he was given command of the Department of Southwestern Virginia and began his raids again but the old fire seemed to have gone. The Confederacy was rapidly on the downgrade and this seemed to be reflected by the excesses which Morgan's raiders committed in these later days. In September, 1864, Morgan was killed in Tennessee while on a raid against the city of Knoxville. The end was in sight and perhaps Stuart and Morgan would not have wished to see it.

Back in Virginia, in the meantime, another cavalry star had risen in the Confederate ranks, in the person of John Singleton Mosby, a steel-nerved, 125-pound wildcat, who probably caused more trouble to the Union army, in proportion to the numbers he led, than any other individual Rebel. Mosby had once entered the University of Virginia but had been expelled for shooting and wounding a fellow student during a dispute and had served a short term in jail. Later he became a lawyer, married, and was on his way to success when war broke out.

Young Mosby enlisted in a mounted rifle company under the command of a salty and profane character, Major "Grumble" Jones, a West Pointer, who had resigned from the army to live a hermit's life in the Virginia mountains. Grumble was decidedly an eccentric but he knew his military drill and Mosby obtained an excellent basic training in cavalry fundamentals. Mosby found the cavalry life to be his forte and soon rose to be adjutant of his regiment, with frequent scouting assignments, which sounds like a strange mixture, but it was a scouting report of his which sent Jeb Stuart off on his daring circuit ride of McClellan's army in June, 1862, and it was Mosby who rode ahead throughout as guide to the column. After this great success, Mosby remained for a while on Jeb Stuart's staff until he was authorized to raise and command a body of Rangers.

*Mosby's Rangers destroying a Union supply train. From Harper's
Weekly and probably by Thomas Nast again. Nast could always
give the other side a raffish touch.*

The Confederate Congress had passed the Partisan Ranger Act during the early stages of the war and this allowed the Rangers to act independently of the regular army and entitled them to all the legitimate loot captured from the enemy. In January, 1863, Mosby began operations with nine Rangers and, within a few days, had terrorized the Federal outposts before Fredericksburg, and captured and paroled twenty-two Yankee troopers, keeping their horses and equipment. Jeb Stuart was delighted and sent him off again with fifteen followers. Again Mosby attacked isolated pickets and harassed small detachments and again returned with much loot. His success and the informality of the Rangers attracted recruits until the command finally consisted of eight companies of cavalry and one of mounted artillery.

The Rangers never camped together at night, each man finding his own quarters among friends in the neighborhood of northwestern Virginia; they lived completely off the country, and all furnished their own equipment. After a fight, they would scatter to the four quarters and meet again later. They had but few carbines and no sabers and depended almost entirely upon their revolvers for weapons. There was no army drudgery, no drills, and plenty of loot, and Mosby's Rangers became a very, very popular organization to join. They freely helped themselves to the personal belongings of their prisoners, and the Federal authorities came to look upon them as robbers and treated them accordingly.

One dark night in March, 1863, Mosby and twenty men slipped into the heart of the Union forces and entered the headquarters of Brigadier General Edwin H. Stoughton, a Vermonter, at Fairfax Court House. Entering the general's bedroom, Mosby found that officer snoring stertorously in bed while several empty champagne bottles scattered about told a story. Mosby awoke the general to sputtering amazement by disrespectfully raising the blankets, then his nightshirt, and spanking him on the behind, and then carried him and one hundred other prisoners with their mounts safely back to the Confederate lines.

Mosby was received with acclaim for this feat and was promoted to major. The daring raids continued and the ire of the Yankees rose proportionately. In the autumn of 1863, he became a sort of unofficial ruler of the extreme tip of northwestern Virginia, which came to be called Mosby's Confederacy. Here he lived with his men as a sort of Robin Hood, meting out justice to the countryside, and billeting his men among a sympathizing people. Often the Union troops invaded this sanctuary to demolish Mosby and his Rangers but it was like trying to fight the morning mist. They hunted Mosby relentlessly and ceaselessly but they never caught him, and he continued to hide in the mountains by day and to descend upon the enemy by night, ever maintaining his high standard of troublemaking. He was almost as much at home inside the Union lines as within his own and, with his uniform covered by a poncho, often hobnobbed with the enemy soldiers or rode along in their supply columns.

The anger of the Union authorities against the unorthodox tactics of Mosby reached such an intensity, and young General George Armstrong Custer (later to die at the Little Big Horn massacre) became so furious at the capture of his messengers and supplies, which had made him more or less ridiculous (and Custer could not stand ridicule) that, with General Grant's approval, he shot and hanged six captured Rangers out of hand. Mosby, soon afterwards, hanged five Federal prisoners, Custer's

men, chosen by lot, in retaliation, and notified General Phil
Sheridan that this would continue — measure for measure — if
this sort of thing went on. It never happened again.

On October 13, 1864, a night train pulled out of Baltimore for
the west. Beyond Harper's Ferry, in Maryland, it suddenly
jolted to an upheaving stop as the engine left the track. A crowd
of gray-clad Rangers boarded the train and, working rapidly,
found two Union army paymasters whom they relieved of
$173,000 in greenbacks, which brought each of the Rangers
about $2100 — Mosby taking nothing, as was his custom. This
particular raid became known as the Greenback Raid, and the

W. H. Carter, Sixth Cavalry.
Harvard College Library

"Captured by Mosby's Guerrillas" — a calmer view of
Mosby's activities

story grew in the telling. The resulting panic among other pay-masters was such that one of them telegraphed Washington from Martinsburg, West Virginia, "I have my funds in the parlor of the United States Hotel here guarded by a regiment."

Mosby was wounded several times and rose to be a colonel before the end of the war. There was some difficulty in his securing the liberal parole terms which Grant had extended to Lee's officers at Appomattox but this was finally adjusted and John Mosby returned to the practice of law. Strangely enough, he became a friend of President Grant and even turned Republican to support him, which caused considerable friction with his old comrades-in-arms. In 1878 he was appointed United States Consul at Hong Kong where he remained for seven years. After that, he turned to lecturing and writing and finally died in 1916.

Mosby was an expert in partisan warfare and a harbinger of the modern commandos, and his reconnaissance and intelligence reports were of the best. His iron nerve, originality, and quickness of wit made him the best of all the guerrilla-type cavalry leaders of the Civil War, and his use of horses for his small bands of fleeting marauders was most effective.

The above four men were probably the best known and most colorful Confederate cavalry leaders although Mosby and Morgan were leaders of partisans and not of regular troops. But there were others of great ability and courage, and possibly of more value than Mosby and Morgan; and it would not be fair to omit mention of Wade Hampton, the wealthy South Carolina plantation owner and grandson of a brigadier general of the War of 1812, who sacrificed all his possessions in the war, became second in command to Jeb Stuart during his zenith, succeeded him at his death, and had to bear the full brunt of the later defeats and discouragements. Hampton was wounded three times during his gallant service and later became a governor of his state and a United States senator.

And there was Turner Ashby who in his short military career of one year had every mark of being the greatest partisan leader of them all. Mark Twain once wrote that the prewar South lived in a romantic dream world based on the novels of Sir Walter Scott. The Virginian, Turner Ashby, with a brigand's mustachios and beard, and the swarthy complexion and fine features of an Arab, looked as if he had stepped out of a Waverly novel. Ashby, like Forrest, was an amateur but a born cavalryman, and in his brief time he made possible the execution of Stonewall Jackson's great plans in the Shenandoah Valley in the spring of 1862. It was Ashby's idea to have fast-moving, horse-drawn light artillery accompany the cavalry, a system which was soon adopted by all. Ashby, riding a superb thoroughbred white stallion, was a symbol of southern romantic ideals and he gave every promise of rivaling Forrest as a natural cavalry genius when he was killed in June, 1862.

Another Confederate cavalryman of ability and note was Fighting Joe Wheeler of Georgia, whose forebears, like those of some other Confederate cavalrymen, came from New England; his father hailed from New Haven, Connecticut. Wheeler had graduated from West Point in 1859 and had served on the frontier with the old 1st Dragoons and Mounted Rifles. He became a lieutenant general in the Confederate Army and commanded the cavalry in the west. He was wounded three times and was said to have taken part in two hundred engagements and eight hundred skirmishes, so that the sobriquet of "Fighting Joe" was certainly fairly earned. After the war, he became a congressman from Louisiana; and during the Spanish-American

War, like Fitzhugh Lee, he came back to the old flag, served as a major general of volunteers, and commanded the cavalry division before Santiago, Cuba.

Then there were the many Lees. At times it seemed as if every other man on horseback in the Confederate Army was named Lee. Besides the great general, there were: Stephen Dill Lee (no relation), who commanded the cavalry west of Alabama; George Washington Custis Lee, eldest son of the general, who served on Jefferson Davis's staff; Fitzhugh Lee, a nephew, an old pre-war regular cavalryman and an extremely able one who served under Stuart and afterwards with great distinction, and later became governor of Virginia and a major general of volunteers during the Spanish-American War; and finally there was William Henry Fitzhugh Lee, the general's second son, called "Rooney" to distinguish him from his cousin, who was educated at Harvard, where his classmate Henry Adams said he showed "the Virginian habit of command." Another classmate, General Horace Porter, said, "Rooney Lee was the best oarsman, I have ever seen, Fitz Lee the best horseman." *

The Confederate cavalry had tremendous color and dash, able and aggressive leaders, and accomplished great things, but it could not overcome the drab and dreary process of attrition which slowly ate into it like a cancer, until nothing remained to fight with.

* The records show that Rooney Lee rowed No. 5 on the Harvard crew of 1857 at a weight of 175 pounds and was the heaviest man in the boat, which averaged 149½ pounds per man. President Emeritus Charles W. Eliot of Harvard wrote of this crew: "In the rowing season of 1857 the recognized Harvard eight-oared crew was heavily defeated by a Boston amateur crew [Union Boat Club] . . . and the accepted reason for the defeat was that certain members of the crew had violated all the rules of the day concerning training, and had in consequence given out during the race" (*The H Book of Harvard Athletics*, 1852–1922 [Cambridge, 1923]).

All of which has nothing whatever to do with the cavalry.

113

"The Courier," by Gilbert Gaul

CHAPTER VI

The Union Cavalry

1861 – 1865

THE FIVE REGULAR mounted regiments in the United States Army were considerably confused at the outbreak of fighting, in April, 1861. The remnants of the 2nd Cavalry finally beat their way back to the East, after the debacle in Texas, but the small detachments of the other four regiments, widely scattered all over the western frontier, were disordered because of the many resignations of officers to join the Confederate cause and because of their distance from events. Most of these units were eventually ordered to abandon their posts and to proceed to the active theaters of war, and a body of the new 2nd Cavalry (formerly the 2nd Dragoons, a change in name which will be explained shortly) rode, under Captain Alfred Pleasonton, all the way from Utah to Washington, D. C., in the autumn of 1861. A few detachments, however, remained at their isolated posts for the duration of the war and became the forgotten men of the conflict. The abandonment of so many frontier posts canceled the hard-won gains made against the hostile Indians through the years and brought on a renewed fury of attacks against the settlements, and it took over twenty years of postwar fighting finally to establish peace and order.

After the fall of Fort Sumter, in April, 1861, President Lincoln issued a call for volunteers and ordered an increase in the regular army which included another mounted regiment, the

3rd Cavalry, to which David Hunter of the 1st Dragoons was appointed colonel, and William H. Emory, of border-surveying fame, the lieutenant colonel.

At the battle of Bull Run (or Manassas) on July 21, 1861, there were seven companies of regular cavalry attached to the Union army of 40,000 men, and these companies stood steady in that dreadful rout and covered well the panicky flight of the volunteers from the field.

The next month, on August 3, Congress passed a bill organizing all the mounted troops — dragoons, mounted riflemen, and cavalry — into one branch, all to be called cavalry and to be numbered by seniority, with the following results, which caused confusion then and have ever since:

Old Name	Date of Origin	New Name
1st Dragoons	1833	1st Cavalry
2nd Dragoons	1836	2nd Cavalry
Mounted Riflemen	1846	3rd Cavalry
1st Cavalry	1855	4th Cavalry
2nd Cavalry	1855	5th Cavalry
3rd Cavalry	1861	6th Cavalry

This changing of names was bad for morale, for the years had accumulated many traditions and much sentiment about the old titles. Also the cavalry yellow was designated as the color of the new corps, and the facings of the other uniforms — orange for the dragoons and green for the riflemen, to which distinctive detail all were strongly attached — were ordered to be changed accordingly. But the usual permission was given to wear out the uniforms on hand, and these achieved a remarkably long life, some even lasting to the end of the war.

These six regular cavalry regiments were soon swamped and lost in a deluge of volunteer mounted regiments which brought

T. F. Rodenbough, From Everglades to Cañon with the Second Dragoons. *Yale University Library*

Sketches of the Second Cavalry — the Old Second Dragoons

the strength of the Union cavalry to about 80,000 men by the end of the war. It would be tedious and useless to follow the course of this handful of regulars during the war, and so we shall temporarily put aside their story until the postwar resumption of Indian fighting in the West.

There were some handicaps to the raising of Union cavalry regiments. The men in the industrial and urban areas of the Northeast were largely office workers or factory laborers who had grown away from the rigors of outdoor life. But the same men, soft as they had become, had one basic virtue which eventually paid off: they were used to a certain amount of discipline and were easier to handle than the highly individualistic Southerners. However, in the states of the Northwest, which still retained a virile residue of the old frontier spirit, the men were more like the Southerners in their knowledge of horses and guns, and it was from this section that some of the best volunteer cavalry regiments were raised.

The organization of the Union cavalry had great inertia. It was much slower in starting than that of the Confederates but when it finally picked up momentum it became a veritable Juggernaut and crushed everything before it. By the end of the war, under the superb leadership of Generals Phil Sheridan and James H. Wilson, it became the best arm of the service and probably the most efficient body of soldiers on earth, and it literally tore the guts out of the Confederate forces. Sheridan's young officers, like Wilson, Judson Kilpatrick, David McMurtrie, George Armstrong Custer, Wesley Merritt, and Ranald Slidell Mackenzie, were like young tigers, and once they tasted blood, they ravened for more.

But for almost two years, the great resources of the North were wasted by incompetence and the cavalry was dissipated by detail. It was initially attached to infantry commands and rather futilely used on petty defensive assignments such as outposts and patrols, as orderlies, messengers, and grooms for staff officers, and as guards for slow-moving wagon convoys which infantry could have done equally well.

It took two years to train a cavalryman, for the duties required a higher order of intelligence and initiative than the other branches, and a good trooper had to be equally efficient mounted or dismounted. The wastage during this time was fabulous. About 284,000 horses were furnished to never more than 60,000 men in the field, which was an average of almost five horses per man, and, as the actual number in the field was usually well below this number, the real wastage was even larger. One swallow too much of water allowed to heated horses on long marches, by the thousands of green Union troopers in the early part of the war, meant losses of millions of dollars — and it happened all the time. It was in things like this that the experienced Confederate horsemen had such an advantage at the start.

Harper's Weekly. *Harvard College Library*

"The Union Forever! — A Cavalry Charge"
Probably by Winslow Homer.

The useless amount of equipment with which the Union trooper weighed down his horse at the beginning was a source of wonder to the light-riding Confederates. Captain Vanderbilt of the 10th New York Cavalry from Elmira, New York, described his first escort duty in December, 1862, as follows: *

> . . . my company had been mustered into the service only about six weeks before, and had received horses less than a month prior to this march; and in the issue we drew everything on the list — watering-bridles, lariat ropes, and pins — in fact, there was nothing on the printed list of supplies that we did not get. Many men had extra blankets, nice large quilts presented by some fond mother or maiden aunt (dear souls), sabres and belts, together with the straps that pass over the shoulders, carbines and slings, pockets full of cartridges, nose bags and extra little bags for carrying oats, haversacks, canteens, and spurs — curry-combs, brushes, ponchos, button tents, overcoats, frying-pans, cups, coffee pots, etc.

After the company mounted, the captain went on:

> Such a rattling, jingling, jerking, scrabbling, cursing, I never heard before. Green horses — some of them had never been ridden — turned round and round, backed against each other, jumped up or stood up like trained circus-horses. Some of the boys had a pile in front on their saddles, and one in the rear, so high and heavy it took two men to saddle one horse and two men to help the fellow into his place. The horses sheered out, going sidewise, pushing the well-disposed animals out of position, etc. Some of the boys had never ridden anything since they galloped on a hobby horse, and they clasped their legs close together, thus unconsciously sticking the spurs into their horses' sides.
>
> Blankets slipped from under saddles and hung from one

* N. D. Preston, History of the Tenth Regiment of Cavalry, New York State Volunteers (New York, 1892) pp. 54–55.

corner; saddles slipped back until they were on the rumps of horses; others turned and were on the under side of the animals; horses running and kicking; tin pans, mess-kettles — flying through the air; and all I could do was to give a hasty glance to the rear and sing out at the top of my voice, "C-L-O-S-E- U-P!"

After just such a purgatory of an initiation like this, the Union troopers were often rushed into action, where they usually fell victims to some roving band of seasoned Confederates who welcomed the chance to appropriate their horses and superior equipment. In fact, the Confederate cavalry depended largely on captured material and mounts to fill its needs.

Besides the enormous losses caused by the Union troopers' inexperience and poor horsemanship, they were usually totally ignorant, at first, about how to care for their horses' backs and feet, and about the proper food and necessary cleanliness for their mounts. But the troopers were not always to blame: there was one case where a shipment of horses was left on freight cars for fifty hours without food or water, and then issued for immediate service.

Gradually some order was brought out of this chaos, and the long delay for many regiments in waiting for equipment and arms was usually given to constant drilling, often mounted on bareback, which eventually brought its reward. The Quartermaster Department established great centers for feed where bales of hay were stored and issued, and six large remount depots were built in convenient localities to furnish horses as needed; and needed they constantly were, for in the fiscal year ending June 30, 1864, the government bought or captured a total of 210,000 horses to supply the army's need for 500 fresh horses a day. Later, Sheridan alone required 150 new horses each day

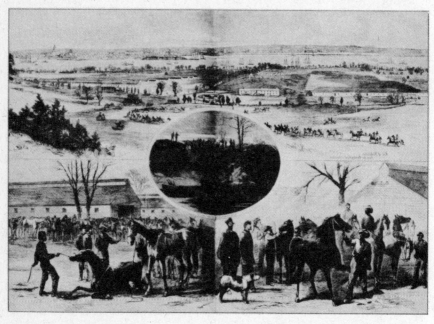

The U. S. cavalry depot at Giesboro, D.C.,
across the Potomac River from Washington

during the Shenandoah campaign. All these animals had to be constantly shod, and a small army of farriers was employed for this purpose. The largest remount depot was at Giesboro, D. C., which was established in July, 1863, and furnished horses to the Army of the Potomac.

Although the Union cavalry stood on the defensive for almost two years, there were some gallant individual efforts to redress the balance. The grand old man of the cavalry, the

Charge of the Fifth Cavalry at Gaines Mill, June 27, 1862.
By W. T. Trego.

veteran Indian fighter Philip St. George Cooke, who was old
enough to be the father of most of the rising crop of Union
cavalry leaders, found time to write and publish (1861) a
Cavalry Tactics which became the standard for the army. He
also saw field service, against his son-in-law Jeb Stuart, as commander of the so-called Cavalry Reserve, a division of two
brigades, in McClellan's army during the ill-fated Peninsula
Campaign. During the Battle of Gaines Mill on June 27, 1862,

he ordered the regular 5th Cavalry, which numbered but 220 sabers, to charge the advancing Confederate infantry, which it did at a cost of fifty-five casualties. As Cooke's young aide, Wesley Merritt, described it, "the daring charge of the cavalry . . . prevented . . . the capture or dispersion of Fitz John Porter's command." Cooke saw no further field service after this campaign but served well in noncombat positions for the rest of the war and lived on until 1895.

The Union cavalry certainly had its organizational ups and downs as well, largely depending on the prejudices of the various commanding generals. Old General Winfield Scott, veteran of the War of 1812 and the Mexican War, in his seventy-sixth year, had nominal command at the outbreak of the war and believed that cavalry would be "unimportant and secondary" against the new rifled cannons in the broken and wooded country between the North and South. George Brinton McClellan, however, who succeeded Scott, was an old cavalryman who, it will be remembered, had served on the frontier with the old 1st Cavalry and had later designed the famous McClellan saddle. "Little Mac" was a great organizer, if not an aggressive fighter, and he understood the proper functions of mounted troops, which he well called the antennae of an army; but he was relieved before he could realize his plan of assigning one regiment of cavalry to each division and forming a reserve of the regulars and some picked volunteer cavalry regiments for the Army of the Potomac in the East. His successor, John Pope, was crushed at the Second Battle of Bull Run (or Manassas) because of the Confederate superiority in this arm which left him like a man groping in the dark. McClellan came back for a while after Pope to command the Army of the Potomac but was again relieved and no progress was made in grouping the cavalry into a compact corps until Joseph Hooker took command. In the West, it was much the same story, for General Rosecrans's cavalry remained inferior to that of General Joe Wheeler, despite Rosecrans's urgent pleas for reinforcements in the mounted arm which, however, the War Department refused to heed. It took time and sad experience to awaken the powers that were in Washington — and some of the generals.

By the spring of 1863, the Union cavalry finally got rolling when Colonel Benjamin H. Grierson of the Illinois Volunteers led the first large and successful raid into Confederate territory,

Harvard College Library

"Surprise of Rebel Guerrillas by a Squadron of United States Cavalry." By Thomas Nast for Harper's Weekly.

after two long years of waiting and watching the Confederate cavalry gain the glory and the loot. Grierson left La Grange, Tennessee, on April 17, 1863, with a brigade of Illinois and Iowa cavalry, about 2000 men, and cut a swath of havoc southward through Mississippi, burning and destroying Confederate supplies, railways, and bridges, and then rode on to the Louisiana capital, Baton Rouge, after having marched three hundred miles without any loss. The raid was a huge success and a great encouragement to the Union cavalry, but it was much aided by Streight's simultaneous raid into Alabama, which ended in failure and surrender to Nathan Forrest. The latter did not have the resources to cope with both raids. These raids had the additional purposes of distracting attention from General Grant's successful venture of passing his army across the Mississippi River from Arkansas to the east side below Vicksburg. Grierson reported after his arrival at Baton Rouge that he had found the heart of the Confederacy but a hollow shell with all the able-bodied men away on the battle line.

Another large Union cavalry raid was made in the East, at the same time, when General George Stoneman, whom we first met on Philip St. George Cooke's Mormon expedition, and young Colonel Judson Kilpatrick, of New York, raided to the rear of Lee's army in northern Virginia. The raid in itself was a success but it proved ill timed and a major strategic error for General Joseph Hooker, because the absence of these troops as a cavalry screen allowed Stonewall Jackson to march unobserved around Hooker's right flank and to fall upon that unsuspecting general with disastrous results at Chancellorsville.

In June, 1863, the Federal cavalry, under Alfred Pleasonton, an old dragoon and Mexican War veteran, fought the bloody Battle of Brandy Station with Jeb Stuart's corps, the first time

*"Gallant charge of the Sixth New York Cavalry" at
Brandy Station, Virginia, October 11, 1863*

the Union force had slugged it out on about equal terms with
the enemy. The following month, Pleasonton commanded the
Union cavalry at Gettysburg where John Buford, another old
dragoon, selected the place, opened the battle, and held back
the Confederates until the Union infantry arrived — which has
been called the most valuable day's work done by the cavalry
in the Civil War. Later, as the battle developed, these two, with
Custer and Gregg, prevented Jeb Stuart from reaching the
Union rear while Pickett was making his famous frontal charge.

Colonel Judson Kilpatrick's raid into Virginia

The next big Union cavalry raid was made in February-March, 1864, under the command of the fiery young New Yorker, Judson Kilpatrick, a classmate of Custer's at West Point. Both these young daredevils were out to make a name for themselves at all costs and both rose to the temporary rank of major general during the war, Custer before his twenty-fifth birthday. This raid had the rather visionary purpose of freeing the thousands of Federal prisoners who were rotting away in the squalor of Libby Prison and Belle Isle, just outside Richmond. Kilpatrick was accompanied by Colonel Ulric Dahlgren of New York, a twenty-two-year-old firebrand, who had already lost a leg in the Gettysburg campaign and who was the son of Admiral John Adolph Dahlgren, the famous naval ordnance officer. Kilpatrick led about 4000 men, and detached five hundred of these under Dahlgren to attack Richmond from the south. This little detachment was ambushed, its leader killed, and Kilpatrick was forced to withdraw when he found the Confederate capital prepared for his attack. It was a gallant attempt, which came within five miles of Richmond — the nearest any Union troops came to that city before its fall.

In April, 1864, the real turn into the home stretch to victory came when Philip Sheridan was placed in command of all cavalry of the Army of the Potomac. Little Phil, as his men called him, may have been short in stature but he became the giant and the genius of the Union cavalry. Born to a poor Irish immigrant family, probably in Albany, New York, he had graduated from West Point in 1853, after a year's suspension for threatening a cadet officer, while forming for drill, with his bayonet, and afterwards for trying to beat up this same superior in front of the barracks, with the unfortunate result that he was beaten up himself. But that was Phil Sheridan. He would fight anybody, anywhere, at the drop of a hat. After graduation, he had served as an infantry officer on the frontier and had risen to the rank of captain at the outbreak of the war. He served then as quartermaster for General Halleck in Missouri, a staff and desk job which he loathed with every ounce of his combative soul, but finally was appointed colonel of a Michigan volunteer cavalry regiment in May, 1862, and came into his own. By the end of that year he had risen to be a major general. He later won distinction at Chickamauga and at Missionary Ridge at Chattanooga which brought him high favor with

Grant and led to his transfer to the eastern theater to command the Cavalry Corps, then about 10,000 men, of the Army of the Potomac.

Sheridan was, above all things, a fighter. A short man of abrupt speech, rather bandy-legged, like Grant, plain in his dress, the first impression he made on a stranger was apt to be unfavorable. It had been so with Grant, but this opinion was quickly reversed by all who were connected with him and the Cavalry Corps soon knew it was led by a supremely capable general. Normally a rather glum and laconic man, he was metamorphosed by the action and excitement of the battlefield, where he cursed and encouraged his men, at the top of his voice, with his flaming vitality. He never, in the end, lost a battle. He had the invincible spirit always to attack after an initial reverse to his own forces, which created a wild enthusiasm among his men, who followed him fanatically, with frenzied confidence in his leadership. The Confederates had several great cavalry leaders, but the Union had one who finally overtopped them all, Philip Henry Sheridan. Sheridan actually had commanded his Michigan cavalry regiment for only a month and seven days, which seems to support the theory, so well exemplified by Nathan B. Forrest, that cavalry leaders are born, not made.

Sheridan reported for duty to General George Meade and immediately ran into difficulties. Years later he wrote in his *Memoirs* of Meade, "He was filled with the prejudices, that from the beginning of the war had pervaded the army regarding the importance and usefulness of cavalry." Sheridan found the men of his new command in good shape and their equipment excellent, but the horses were worn down by what he considered unnecessary patrol duty, from continuously riding a

*Philip H. Sheridan and some of his young cavalry generals.
Left to right: Philip H. Sheridan, James W. Forsyth, Wesley
Merritt, Thomas C. Devin, George A. Custer.*

line of almost sixty miles around the camps of the Army of the Potomac. He told an unbelieving Meade that this continuous, irksome duty by the cavalry was wrong. He wanted to concentrate its strength for attack, and he felt confident he could whip Jeb Stuart, the perennial scourge, if allowed to do so. Meade reported this conversation to Grant, who replied, "Then let him go out and do it." The Union cavalry at last had broken its chains.

Sheridan had found the equipment of his troopers excellent, for the northern factories were turning out a flood of arms, munitions, and general military supplies. The men were furnished light and short carbines of various patterns, the famous Sharp carbine often being replaced by the Spencer, which fired seven rounds with more or less rapidity but which was difficult to reload quickly. A few were armed with the Henry rifle, an improved weapon, which fired sixteen shots with great accuracy; and there also was a Colt's rifle which fired six rounds. All the men carried the Colt's revolver, of the army or navy pattern, which was fired by percussion caps. One Confederate trooper, discouraged by the far superior repeating small arms of his Yankee opponents, asked, "Say, do you all load those guns you all fight with on Sunday, and then fire 'em all the week?"

The long, straight, heavy Prussian sabers which were standard at the beginning of the war had been replaced by the light cavalry saber with a curved blade which could be fixed to the carbines as a bayonet. The McClellan saddle, which had been successfully modified to American requirements, made trouble only when it was covered with rawhide instead of leather, when it became a torture to use if split.

The silly-looking cavalry hat with a bedraggled-looking black ostrich feather, which Albert Brackett had described as "an ungainly piece of furniture," had been succeeded by the trim and practical trooper's forage cap, although the slouch hat was also worn, especially by officers. The field uniform was still the light blue trousers, but with a yellow stripe down the outside seam for all mounted regiments, and a snug short dark blue jacket buttoned to the throat and held in around the waist by a wide leather belt which could support a revolver and saber. Boots were not usually worn except by escort or special details.

The Union cavalry was rarin' to go, once its horses were rested, and Phil Sheridan was the man to lead it.

On the morning of May 9, 1864, while Grant and Lee were pounding each other in the horror of the struggle in the Wilderness, Sheridan's Cavalry Corps moved in column toward Fredericksburg with the expressed purpose of finding Jeb Stuart and fighting it out with him. In the van, General Wesley Merritt, still in his twenties, led his division, and behind rode his equally young classmate of West Point, James Harrison Wilson, with another division, while David M. Gregg, a comparatively old man of thirty-one, headed a third. One of the brigade commanders was George Armstrong Custer, who was in his twenty-fourth year, and all were under the command of Sheridan, who could count thirty-two birthdays. Youth was literally in the saddle.

Jeb Stuart soon discovered this invasion in force and sent Fitzhugh Lee to attack Sheridan's rear. Custer, in the meantime, had defeated an opposing Confederate force and inflicted much damage. On May 11, the two main bodies met head-on at Yellow Tavern, where the young star of the Confederate cavalry, Jeb Stuart, was killed, with a rose in his gray jacket. Sheridan had achieved his objectives by breaking up General Lee's railroad communications, destroying large amounts of vital sup-

133

plies, and defeating Stuart's cavalry, in which a mounted charge of two brigades, led by Custer, had broken the Confederate lines. Sheridan had kept his promise to whip Stuart, and his name and the morale of the Union cavalry soared accordingly.

Sheridan's next move was to clean up the Shenandoah Valley, which had been a natural highway, flanking Washington to the west, for the Confederates on their forays and raids to the north. Its fertile farms were the granary and constant source of supplies for the Confederate forces in northwestern Virginia and it was the bailiwick of John Singleton Mosby and his destructive Rangers. In July, 1864, General Jubal Early had slipped up this funnel to reach the outskirts of Washington and then on to burn Chambersburg, Pennsylvania. The valley was like a rifle barrel aimed at the heart of the North and it was imperative that the aim of this barrel be reversed.

In September, 1864, Sheridan wrote to Grant, "I will go on and clear out the Valley," and on the 19th, at Opequon Creek, he won a victory which drove Early's Confederates "whirling through Winchester," as he telegraphed the news to his jubilant superiors. This success was followed up by constant cavalry aggressions by the two boy generals, Custer and Merritt, and the Union forces pushed on down the Great Valley, destroying the crops and supplies.

But on the morning of October 19, Jubal Early nearly won back all he had lost by a surprise attack on the Union camp at Cedar Creek, with "Sheridan twenty miles away" in Winchester, asleep in bed. Thomas Buchanan Read's rather sentimental and dated poem, "Sheridan's Ride," was once known to every schoolchild, until time and two great world wars somewhat obscured the events and leaders of the Civil War; and parts of it still

134

T. Buchanan Read, Sheridan's Ride. *Drawing
by author. Harvard College Library*

*Sheridan's arrival at Cedar Creek, October 19, 1864. "Hurrah!
hurrah for Sheridan! Hurrah! hurrah! for horse and man!"*

carry the unconquerable spirit of Sheridan and his genius for
turning defeat into victory.

> Up from the South at break of day,
> Bringing to Winchester fresh dismay,
> The affrighted air with a shudder bore,
> Like a herald in haste, to the chieftain's door,
> The terrible grumble, and rumble, and roar,
> Telling the battle was on once more,
> And Sheridan twenty miles away.

And when the general arrived on the battlefield after a mad
dash of twenty miles:

135

The first that the general saw were the groups
Of stragglers, and then the retreating troops.
What was done? What to do? A glance told him both;
Then, striking his spurs, with a terrible oath,
He dashed down the line, 'mid a storm of huzzas,
And the wave of retreat checked its course there, because
The sight of the Master compelled it to pause.

Sheridan's uncanny personal magnetism turned an initial rout into a great victory as the beaten Union troops turned back into the fight with storming confidence. It was not strictly a cavalry battle but the cavalry completed the defeat of Early's troops and captured enormous quantities of supplies, arms, and many hundreds of prisoners. It was a final and complete victory; the Great Valley had been laid waste and no more would support a Confederate force or serve as a chute for raids to the north.

For the rest of the year 1864 Sheridan and his young tigers Merritt, Custer, Devin, and Mackenzie tore away at the remnants of Early's army. A keen rivalry led these young officers to front-line fighting and hand-to-hand encounters at the cannon's mouth. They suffered many wounds, especially Ranald Mackenzie, the youngest of all, who was wounded six times, and, after the war, went on to greater heights on the Indian fighting frontier.

In the spring of 1865, Sheridan reached his peak in the final Appomattox campaign. He returned in March with three cavalry divisions to the Army of the Potomac to join Grant before Petersburg, Virginia, where he received orders to destroy the railroads which still supplied Lee's dwindling forces. By the end of the month, Sheridan had left Lee with but one railroad open. In early April, General Wesley Merritt led a concentration of Union cavalry at Five Forks which again defeated the Confederates, ruined Lee's avenue of retreat from Richmond to Danville, and forced him to evacuate Petersburg for the last march to Appomattox. As Lee's harassed army struggled westward in its death throes, the Union cavalry scourged it with dismounted fire from behind cover, and then each unit would mount and gallop down the line of retreat to dismount and resume their murderous fire as Lee's tortured legions staggered into range. Finally Sheridan's men were thrown squarely across the van of the desperate army. Then Lee knew it was all over and rode to Appomattox for the surrender.

In the meantime, the Union cavalry had also been furiously active in the western theaters of the war. General Sherman chose the New York Irish firebrand, Judson Kilpatrick, to lead his cavalry on his march to Atlanta, and afterwards to the sea and northward. He called Kilpatrick "a crazy damn fool" who was just the reckless madcap needed to screen his daring march through the heart of the Confederacy, cut off from all supplies and contacts. Kilpatrick led four divisions, about 15,000 sabers, until the capture of Atlanta, and then accompanied Sherman from there on his famous march to the sea with one division of 5000 troopers.

In October, 1864, another master cavalryman, second only to Sheridan, rose in the West. General James H. Wilson, who had commanded one of Sheridan's cavalry divisions in the Shenandoah campaign, and had previously been in charge of the Cavalry Bureau in Washington, was made Chief of Cavalry of the Military Division of the Mississippi, which placed him on a practical equality with Sheridan. Like the other Union cavalry leaders, he was young, having graduated from West Point in 1860, and was only twenty-seven when he became a major

137

general of volunteers in 1864. Wilson was a born organizer and a man of great flexibility who emphasized the importance of his men's ability to adapt themselves to circumstances so that they could fight equally well mounted or dismounted. In the Battle of Nashville in December, 1864, his mounted men had gained a position to the rear of the enemy and then, dismounting, had gallantly stormed a Confederate breastwork, side by side with the infantry, which was the decisive blow for victory; and this quick versatility marked his men. The Confederate general Hood said of this attack that it was the first and only time he beheld a Confederate army abandon the field in confusion.

The next year, in March, 1865, young General Wilson made his famous raid through Alabama, the largest and most successful cavalry raid of the war. It was really more than a raid — it was an invasion by an army of cavalry, a preview of a blitzkrieg. Wilson had given much time to the drilling and equipment of his command and it was a superbly armed and disciplined force of about 14,000 men which set out from Tennessee. Most of his men were armed with the new Spencer repeating carbine, which gave them many times the fire power of the opposing Confederates under Forrest. Everything had been planned for mobility, and each trooper carried five days' rations, one hundred rounds of ammunition, and even extra horseshoes. Pack animals bore additional rations, and a supply train of 250 wagons furnished enough additional supplies for a sixty-day campaign. A light pontoon train of thirty boats was also brought along. Never before or since has such a splendid cavalry command been seen in the entire Western Hemisphere.

Wilson pushed forward in constant skirmishes against Forrest's scattered and war-worn troops, who, although about equal in numbers, were equipped with inferior arms, and consequently were pushed aside or overwhelmed in their desperate twilight stand for the Confederacy by this precursor of a modern, mobile, blitz army.

Wilson, to a certain extent, stole Forrest's thunder in this invasion by getting there first with the most. Besides his superior mobility, armament, and the training of his men, which enabled them to meet infantry in stand-up action, he had the advantage of an unknown objective. He fanned his men out over the many

National Archives

General James H. Wilson

different roads leading south and forced Forrest to disperse his men on a broad front for defense. Wilson luckily captured some papers showing the disposition of the Confederates and, rapidly concentrating the bulk of his forces, he overwhelmed a weak enemy division on his left. Forrest was handicapped by the rivers which flowed north and south and so delayed east-and-west movements to unite his men.

Wilson arrived triumphantly before Selma, Alabama, a strongly fortified and most important supply depot of the Confederates, on April 2; and, dismounting his troopers, he carried the city by storm and completely routed the defenders. After destroying all the foundries, arsenals, and stores of every kind, and after replenishing his own needs, he led his mounted men on to Montgomery where he again destroyed all the enemy stores. From there he pushed on into Georgia where he captured Columbus, West Point, and Macon. At the latter place he received news of Lee's surrender at Appomattox and of President Jefferson Davis's flight toward the southwest. He immediately sent out a force to intercept the fleeing Confederate president and, on May 10, this detachment captured him at Irwinsville, Georgia. Wilson's whole march, the longest and largest cavalry march of the war, was an extraordinary operation and recalled the colorful campaigns of the Crusaders, where a mounted army would dismount to attack a fortified position. It was a striking example of the versatility and power of a properly used force of mounted riflemen, in which horses were used for mobility and the actual fighting usually done while dismounted.

Wilson's later military career was blocked by the enmity of President Andrew Johnson with whom he had carried on a bitter feud while Johnson was war governor of Tennessee. Wilson had come to that state, before the Battle of Nashville, to take command of General George Thomas's cavalry but had found there only 5000 available mounts, because Governor Johnson had raised twelve local cavalry regiments, an act which Wilson previously, as head of the Cavalry Bureau, had rejected. Wilson found these men, whom he called a bunch of drunken rowdies, scattered uselessly near their homes, on the Federal payroll, to make votes for Johnson. He at once ordered them to duty with other northern regiments and court-martialed many absent officers. Then he secured authority from Secretary of War Stanton to requisition all horses south of the Ohio River and let the owners sue the government later. He took the horses from the Nashville cabs and streetcars and even attached Governor Johnson's fine stable of horses. There was an acrimonious interview between the two men in which Wilson spoke his mind freely. Later, when Johnson became president, he refused to advance Wilson, even stripped him of his brevet rank, and ordered him to permanent duty as a captain of Engineers. At that point Wilson resigned his commission. He has aptly been called the forgotten man of the Civil War; yet he lived on until 1925, as a successful civil engineer and author, and re-entered the army for a while to serve as a major general in the Spanish-American War and the Boxer Rebellion in China.

The youth of the cavalry leaders of the war was remarkable, especially on the Union side. During World War II, the Air Force officers were proverbially young, but none of them compared with the boy cavalry generals of the Civil War. Jeb Stuart and Phil Sheridan were in their early thirties, while Wesley Merritt, George A. Custer, and Ranald S. Mackenzie were major generals of volunteers before their twenty-fifth birthdays. This latter trio went on to greater fame in the wild postwar days of Indian fighting on the frontier, and we shall meet them again.

141

CHAPTER VII

Back to the Frontier—Sioux and Cheyennes

1865 – 1877

At the end of the Civil War, in April, 1865, things were in frightful shape on the western frontier and along the Mexican border, for the Indians had taken full advantage of the distractions of the conflict and had loosed a fury of attacks against the settlements. In Minnesota and Dakota Territory, the Sioux, under the leadership of Little Crow, who preached the triumph of the Confederacy, had massacred nearly 1000 white settlers in 1862 before a volunteer force defeated them. The Utes had gone on the war path in Idaho; and Kit Carson had led a volunteer force against the rampaging Navajos in New Mexico. The Apaches had crisscrossed Arizona with trails of blood. In Texas matters were even worse, for the Confederate troops, after sporadically occupying the old frontier forts, had largely abandoned them, and the dreaded Comanches and Apaches were again raiding into the outskirts of San Antonio and beyond to the east. All the constructive toil of the army between 1848 and 1861 had been practically undone. To add to these troubles the armies of Maximilian, emperor of Mexico, who had been placed on the throne by the French emperor, Napoleon III, despite the protests of our embattled government, controlled the Mexican side of the Rio Grande and harbored all fleeing Confederates

T. F. Rodenbough, From Everglades to Cañon with
the Second Dragoons. *Yale University Library*

*Cavalry uniforms — mostly dress — during the 1870's, showing the
spiked dress helmet with a yellow horsehair plume which was
worn from 1872 to 1900*

with open arms. The welcome peace after Appomattox focused
attention on these distant troubles which had been obscured
by nearer and more vital events.

So critical were conditions on the Mexican border that
General Phil Sheridan was rushed to Texas in May, 1865, with a
sizable body of troops. These included a Michigan volunteer
cavalry regiment under Major General George A. Custer, which
went to Hempstead, and another mounted regiment under
General Wesley Merritt, which rode to San Antonio. This display of force encouraged the Mexican Liberals, led by Juarez,
who then made fresh efforts to overcome the foreign ruler; and,
aided by strong diplomatic pressure from Washington, they
were successful in overthrowing Maximilian, so that this threat
was at least removed by 1867.

Congress finally realized that, as the huge volunteer army of the late war was demobilized, there was urgent need for a larger regular army, and especially for more cavalry, to mend the damages of the neglected frontier. So in July, 1866, four more cavalry regiments were authorized, the 7th through 10th. Of these, the 9th and 10th were to be made up of Negro enlisted men with white officers. The companies or troops of these regiments numbered twelve each, making 120 serviceable cavalry troops which were usually scattered, as before the war, in splinter fragments all over the frontier.

The cavalry, like the other branches of the service, got its share, for a while, of occupation duty in the southern states during reconstruction — a dirty job which nobody relished, for the enforcement of civil laws, especially when those laws were harsh and often unreasonable, was not to the taste of men who had joined the army for action and adventure. The cavalry, however, was too much in demand on the frontier to be held for long on this kind of assignment and soon it was back in the West, much to the satisfaction of all, for it has been said that "every cavalryman is at heart a Westerner."

This post-Civil war army was unique and came to be known in later days as the "Old Army." Every officer above the grade of second lieutenant was a veteran of the recent war and, of course, most of them took drastic cuts in rank from their wartime status. Many officers also came back as enlisted men, drink often being the impelling reason; and many Confederate ex-officers, who were barred from holding commissions, enlisted in the ranks. Others simply became bored and restless with civilian life when they found their girls had married some stay-at-home, or that jobs were hard to find, or dull with indoor routine if available. The enlisted men were a hard-bitten crowd

144

and on paydays it was considered normal for at least ten per-
cent of a command to land in the guardhouse. At Fort Clark,
Texas, a particularly lonely and rough post, where service was
considered the equivalent to "honorable mention," about
twenty-five per cent of the men would regularly end in the
clink on charges ranging from drunkenness to attempted rape
and murder. But these same men were usually splendid in the
field and the problem was to keep them occupied and away
from the miserable sinkholes of vice which fringed the outskirts
of the frontier posts.

One of these postwar officers was Captain Gerald Russell
of the 3rd Cavalry, born in Kerry, Ireland, who had won a promotion from the ranks by great gallantry and general good
qualities since his original enlistment in the old Mounted Rifles.
Russell had no education and refused to master the elementary
things but spent much time in studying advanced topics in
science and history, with a resulting jumble of ideas delivered
in a brogue rich as cream. John W. Bourke, who became an
ethnologist of some note and wrote well of his army experiences,
was at the time a lieutenant in Russell's troop and reported as
follows a sort of fight talk which his captain gave to a batch of
new recruits:

> Young Min! I conghratulate yiz on bein assigned to moi
> thrupe, becos praviously to dis toime, I vinture to say that moi
> thrupe had had more villins, loyars, teeves, scoundhrils and, I
> moight say, dam murdhrers than enny udder thrupe in de
> United States Ormy. I want yiz to pay sthrict attintion to jooty
> — and not become dhrunken vagabonds, wandhrin all over the
> face of God's Chreashun, spindin ivry cint ov yur pay with low
> bum-mers. Avoide all timptashuns, loikwoise all discipashuns,
> so that in toime yez kin become non-commissioned offizurs;
> yez'll foind yer captin a very laynent man and very much

given to laynency, fur Oi niver duz toi no man up bee der tumbs unless he duz bee late for a roll-call. Sarjint, dismiss de detachment.*

The good captain was at times disappointed in the results and once declared:

I decleer to God'l'moity! The base ingratoichude of dem wearies [his name for the enlisted men] of moine is perficly 'stonishin! . . . they hev just smashed a bran new skillit over my nice first Sarjint's head'n all becoz dey didn't hev enough toe-ma-tusses in dere God-dam supe!

Life for the women of a frontier post was unbelievably crude and hard, and the devotion and loyalty which those truly gallant wives showed to their husbands and their way of life has become a byword. In the North the winters were long, cold, and lonely, and at some of the Mexican border posts there were six months of frightful heat when the thermometer stood at 110 degrees in the shade and life was simply endured during the long searing days when it seemed as if the sun was in one's lap. At Fort Clark, the huge post which protected Texas from raids from the west and south, ice was almost unknown, for it cost six dollars for a small piece packed in sawdust and sent by express from San Antonio. Butter was like oil and the milk was thin and watery and tasted of wild garlic. Beef was dry and had a strange, musty flavor. There were no fresh vegetables and the potatoes shipped in were usually a mass of decay when unpacked. It was impossible to raise flowers, for the sun's heat burned the outer petals. Only the Madeira vine would grow, and this shaded the verandas on which the hapless officers' wives lay on hammocks in the scantiest of clothes and passed the time by exchanging grievances with a visiting neighbor. To

* *The New Mexico Historical Review,* January, 1934.

add to the general exhaustion, a profusion of snakes, scorpions, tarantulas, centipedes, and giant roaches made the summer exciting for the young wife, especially if she had recently arrived from the effete East. Picnics, even after nightfall, were impossible, for the ants, woodticks, and red bugs or chiggers soon ate more of the picnickers than the latter did of any food. To add to the gaiety, quarters were allotted by rank, and if a new married officer arrived or a bachelor married it might mean a general shifting of quarters all down the line, with some poor devil of a second lieutenant and his wife and children ending up in a tent. Many wives could not take it and returned to civilization or persuaded their husbands to resign. But those who remained could face anything.

But it was not all bad — even on the scorching border. The winters there were far different. Then game abounded and venison and wild turkey were plentiful and the sweet potato thrived. There was usually good fishing and discreet bathing in a nearby creek and the days were pleasant and temperate. Then the garrison came to life and there were many balls, masquerades, and theatricals in a gay and friendly atmosphere. The band played for the dances and gave frequent concerts, or it could be hired for serenades. Canvas was spread on the ground for dancing and lanterns lit up the festivities. All single girls quickly married and it was well known that problem spinster relations were brought on — and were usually proposed to by platoons, so great was the demand for wives among the lonely younger officers.

The administration of Indian affairs was in the hands of the Indian Bureau of the Department of the Interior and the differences and disputes between this bureau and the army were endless. Treaties were made with the Indians and broken by all

147

concerned. The Indian Bureau blamed the army and vice versa. But no matter who was to blame, the army always had to go in and clean up the mess and the cavalry, as usual, bore the major share against the mounted Indians.

A big factor in the Indian unrest was the building of the Union Pacific Railroad which cut through the heart of the buffalo range country and was completed to the coast in 1869. This brought in a horde of commercial buffalo hunters, who slaughtered the animals by the thousands for their hides, which were sold in the eastern market for robes and overcoats. The extermination of the buffalo became a grim threat to the wandering tribes, for that animal was more than the staff of life to them: it was life itself! The Indians relied upon it for their food, they got their shelter and clothing from its hide and their tools from its ribs and bones. With the buffalo gone, the way of life of the mounted Indians of the Great Plains was finished — and well they knew it.

Before the completion of the railroad, hostilities broke out all over the West, not at first by any large body of Indians, but in constant small raids. Each of these meant a pursuit by cavalry if possible, and, if detachments of that harassed branch were not available, by the infantry. The whole frontier became in a constant state of alarm and General Phil Sheridan, who commanded the Military Division of the Missouri, said, "Were I or the department commanders to send guards to every point where they are clamored for, we would need alone on the plains a hundred thousand men, mostly of cavalry."

In 1866, a wagon road was started from Fort Laramie, in southeastern Wyoming, to Virginia City, Montana, where gold had been discovered, which ran roughly northwest through the heart of the Sioux country. About one hundred miles up this road,

Fort Phil Kearny was established and garrisoned by five companies of infantry and one of the 2nd Cavalry. In December, Captain W. J. Fetterman incautiously led out a work party, eighty-three strong, which was ambushed by the Sioux Indians, under the leadership of Red Cloud, and killed to the last man. Other attacks followed and the road was finally abandoned and the forts dismantled by a treaty made with the Sioux in the autumn of 1868 which gave that tribe exclusive hunting rights in the disputed area. This well-meant treaty was probably a blunder for it simply confirmed the Indians' belief that they could whip the army and thereby opened up the floodgates of further resistance. The Sioux at this time numbered some 50,000, of whom 8000 were warriors, and were by far the most powerful hostile tribe.

The mainstays of Indian opposition were the Sioux-Cheyennes in the north, the Apaches in Arizona and New Mexico, and in Texas and the Indian Territory (now part of Oklahoma) the Comanches, Kiowas, Arapahoes, and Southern Cheyennes. From over the Mexican border, the Lipans and Kickapoos (often joined by the Comanches and Apaches) added their raids to the general reign of terror. The different tribes varied in their methods of fighting. The Apaches, who were never expert horsemen like the other tribes, could cover fifty to seventy-five miles a day on foot; or they used a sort of mounted infantry technique, riding their horses for swift transportation and then dismounting to fight on foot. The Sioux, Cheyennes, and Comanches, however, fought on horseback, somewhat like the old Mongols or the Cossacks, charging at the enemy in extended order, then, if the foe did not stampede, circling rapidly around him, firing guns, or, what was often more effective under these tactics, arrows, while clinging to the far side of their

149

horses for protection. They would fire, feint a charge, and, when the opportunity offered, drive it home. Individually they were usually better horsemen and shots than their soldier enemies and were only beaten by superior organization and equipment. General George Crook said, "The Sioux is a cavalry soldier from the time he has intelligence enough to ride a horse, or fire a gun. . . . Even with their lodges and families, they can move at the rate of fifty miles a day." The Plains Indians were pronounced by another experienced officer "the finest light cavalry in the world," and still another said, "the Sioux of the Northern Plains were foemen far more to be dreaded than any European cavalry."

There were nearly a hundred tribes, probably between two and three hundred thousand Indians in the million square miles, roughly about one third of the United States, which had to be patrolled and kept in order by about 5000 troops.

Space again forbids a detailed account of the activities of our Indian-fighting cavalry for it would take volumes to relate the skirmishes which continually went on in this period. There was fighting every year from 1865 through 1890, and besides the constant skirmishes there were eleven distinct Indian wars large enough to warrant specific battle honors on the various regimental colors. All these wars were interspersed with innumerable councils and treaties with the Indians but it was force and force alone which finally brought lasting peace.

The whole savage West was aflame, then, after the end of the Civil War, and the Cheyennes, an extraordinarily able tribe in warfare, were especially destructive and hostile. They had a real grievance and were avenging it. A band of the Southern Cheyennes had peacefully sought protection from the authorities at Fort Lyon, Colorado (near the old Bent's Fort on the upper Arkansas River where Stephen Kearny's Army of the West had gathered in 1846 before invading New Mexico), and had settled nearby at Sand Creek. In November, 1864, the 2nd Colorado Cavalry arrived under the command of Colonel J. M. Chivington, a fanatical ex-preacher, who must have been a homicidal maniac and who said, "Kill and scalp all [Indians] big and little; nits make lice." They fell without warning on this unoffending community, although it was under the protection of Major Wynkoop of Fort Lyon, and ruthlessly murdered three hundred Indians, of whom only seventy-five were warriors, the rest being women and children.

General Nelson A. Miles later called it in his *Personal Recollections* "perhaps the foulest and most unjustifiable crime in the annals of America."

So it can be seen why the Cheyennes were out for blood; and under the leadership of Roman Nose, a giant of a man, they were reaping it in western Kansas and Colorado.

Just to show what was going on, the following report of Indian outrages for the first week only of September, 1868, is quoted verbatim from the *Record of Engagements with Hostile Indians* published in Chicago, 1882, by the Headquarters Military Division of the Missouri, Lieutenant General P. H. Sheridan, Commanding (and this week was not particularly worse than many others):

September 1st, near Lake Station, J. H. Jones, stage agent, reported a woman and child killed and scalped and thirty head of stock run off by Indians; at Reed's Springs, three persons were killed and three wounded; at Spanish Fort, Texas, four persons were murdered, eight scalped, fifteen horses and mules run off and three women outraged; one of these three women was outraged by thirteen Indians who afterwards killed and scalped her and then killed her four little children.

September 2nd, on Little Coon Creek, Kansas, a wagon, guarded by four soldiers, commanded by Sergeant Dixon, Company "A," 3rd Infantry, were attacked by about forty Indians. Three of the men were badly wounded; three Indians were killed and one wounded. . . .

September 4th, Major Tilford, 7th Cavalry, Commanding Fort Reynolds, Colorado, reported four persons killed, the day before, near Colorado City. A large body of Indians also attacked the station at Hugo Springs, but were repulsed by the guards.

September 5th, Indians drove off five head of stock from Hugo Springs and then went off and burned Willow Springs station.

September 6th and 7th, twenty-five persons were killed in Colorado, and on the 7th, Hon. Schuyler Colfax [elected Vice-President the following November] telegraphed: "Hostile Indians have been striking simultaneously at isolated settlements in Colorado, for a circuit of over two hundred miles."

Something had to be done and quickly! No regular cavalry were available at the time or place, so Major George A. Forsyth, of the 9th Cavalry, who had ridden with Sheridan from Winchester to turn defeat into victory, and Lieutenant Frederick H. Beecher, a nephew of the famous Brooklyn minister, Henry Ward Beecher, collected fifty civilian frontiersmen and scouts, of which a good number were Union and Confederate veterans (the acting first sergeant, William H. H. McCall of Pennsylvania, had been a Union brigadier general), and started out to trail Roman Nose and his murderous band in September, 1868. Each volunteer was armed with a seven-shot Spencer repeating rifle and a Colt's revolver, and all were mounted. Four mules carried camp equipment, medical supplies, shovels, and 4000 extra rounds of ammunition. Each man carried seven days' rations.

This party of scouts hit the Indians' trail which they followed to the Arickaree Fork of the Republican River in Colorado, just over the border from the extreme northwestern corner of Kansas. On the sixth day, with their rations nearly gone, they encamped on the bank of the nearly dry river. The next morning the Indians suddenly attempted to stampede the party's horses. Hundreds and hundreds of savages appeared upon the surrounding hills, and Forsyth hastily led his small band to an island in the partially dry river bed where they formed a circle and dug in, using the horses — which were gradually all killed — as a sort of breastworks. The Indian warriors in their hundreds made several thunderous charges up the river bed at the island but were repulsed at each assault, although one brave actually rode straight through the defenders. It was later estimated that about 1000 Sioux and Cheyenne warriors took part in the battle, encouraged by the notes of a bugle, probably blown by some army renegade. Those Indians not taking part in the charges kept up a steady fire from all sides. Forsyth was in agony from a bullet in his right thigh, a second which had smashed his left leg, and a third which had torn his scalp. Beecher was killed and about one half of the men were killed or wounded.

The grand climax came when Roman Nose, in all his six feet four inches of superb painted savagery and wearing a magnificent war bonnet, trotted into sight at the head of his massed warriors around a bend in the river, some two miles downstream, for a final charge. The captured bugle blew and a solid mass of screaming Indians broke into a full gallop which swept up the river bed like an approaching wave. The defenders fired five volleys without noticeably checking the impetus of the on-

"Roman Nose's Final Charge At Beecher's Island,"
by Rufus F. Zogbaum

rushing avalanche, but on the sixth, Roman Nose, out in front, fell mortally wounded from his horse, and the scouts standing to deliver, almost point blank, the last shot in their rifles, beat back the Indians, confused by the death of their leader. For the next nine days the living, wounded, and dead huddled together on the island, living on putrid horseflesh seasoned with gunpowder, and on wild plums, and withstood a tight siege, in the stifling heat of the days and the cold of the September nights, from the surrounding Indians who kept up a constant fire. Four men finally slipped successfully through the Indian lines and summoned help, and two troops of the colored 10th Cavalry, who had met a pair of these messengers, came at the gallop to rescue the delirious and tormented survivors. It was truly an epic stand. Forsyth needed a year to recover and later rose to be a brevet brigadier general.

Nearly eight years later, in the mid-afternoon of June 25, 1876, a horde of yelping and screaming Sioux and Cheyenne braves swarmed exultantly over a ridge near the Little Big Horn River in southern Montana to scalp, mutilate, or strip the bodies of Lieutenant Colonel George Armstrong Custer and 212 officers and men of the 7th Cavalry who had died with him in that fantastic and mysterious battle which seems to typify to many Americans the fighting of all our Indian wars.

Probably no other American battle is known better by name and less by fact than "Custer's Last Fight," as it is called on a garish and gory chromo of which over 200,000 copies have been distributed by a brewery to barrooms throughout the length and breadth of the United States. Professor Robert Taft of the University of Kansas, the leading authority on the pictorial record of the Old West, believes this picture has been gazed upon by more lowbrows and fewer art critics than any other

Probably the most discussed picture in the United States,
"Custer's Last Fight," by Cassilly Adams

painting in this country, and, if not the best liked of all American pictures, it has doubtless been the most extensively examined and discussed. A careful survey of the lithograph, as Professor Taft says, is enough to give a sensitive soul a nightmare for a week.* Troopers are being brained, scalped, stripped; soldiers, Indians, and horses are dying by the dozen; Custer with flowing red tie and long golden ringlets is about to deal a terrible saber blow to an advancing Indian who in turn is

* *The Kansas Historical Quarterly,* November, 1946.

"Custer's Todes-Ritt." A German conception of Custer's last stand. Custer and his men are shown fighting mounted with sabers.

shot by a dying trooper. (Custer actually had his hair close-cropped at the time and no sabers were used.) It is a scene of utter confusion and bloody carnage. Probably, through the years, many a well-meaning imbiber who has tarried too long with his foot on the rail and his eye on the picture has almost jumped out of his skin at the sudden yell of a passing newsboy. Its effect on the popular imagination is incalculable, and it unquestionably has helped to make Custer's name the best known of all our Indian-fighting soldiers and perhaps, next to Grant and Lee, the most famous of all our army officers of the nineteenth century.

The controversy and the mystery of Custer's sudden and violent departure to Valhalla with all his men has kept the subject very much alive; nobody knows exactly what happened on that sun-baked ridge, for the only survivor was a horse named "Comanche," who lived on for years afterwards as the pampered pet of the 7th Cavalry. If Custer had defeated the Sioux and Cheyenne hordes on that scorching June afternoon, he would probably have been a hero for a time — and then his victory might well have merged into the background of other successful Indian battles and been forgotten. The unexpected shock of this greatest Indian victory over the white man made a world-wide sensation at the time and the repercussions have been kept alive, not only by the gory chromo, but also by western novels, Hollywood movies, and a never-ending disagreement among writers, historians, and military experts, real and self-appointed. It is a highly controversial affair; and the full details are much too complicated and contentious for the pages of this book.

The central figure of this tragic drama, George Armstrong Custer, went from the foot of his graduating class (1861) at West Point to a major generalcy in the Civil War before his twenty-fifth birthday, probably because of his fearlessness. He was afraid of nothing and would have charged into the gates of Hell if he had had the chance. Five times was he brevetted for gallantry during that war and he rose to his supreme height during its last days, just before the surrender at Appomattox, when he harassed Lee's heroic and exhausted army on its attempted retreat to the west. Custer gave it no rest during that desperate march but hewed away with his cavalrymen at the stumbling column, day and night, darting in at every oppor-

Major General George Armstrong Custer during the Civil War

tunity, to capture men and equipment, making it halt and deploy, and finally throwing his whole mounted division across its path and holding it until the Union infantry could come up in force and, facing eastward, block that last dying attempt to break clear.

After the war, when the four new mounted regiments were authorized in 1866, Custer, who had reverted to the rank of lieutenant colonel, was given actual command of the 7th Cavalry, for its nominal colonel was consistently away on detached service. He made this regiment a crack outfit with great *esprit de corps,* by constant drilling, field work, hand-picked recruits, by his magnetism and untirable energy, and by much martial music by its excellent mounted band. Custer loved martial music and the band usually rode with the regiment in the field. Two airs were the favorites: "The Girl I Left Behind Me," and "Garry Owen," which became the regimental song and starts off with the inviting words:

> Let Bacchus' sons be not dismayed
> But join with me each jovial blade;
> Come booze and sing, and lend your aid,
>   To help me with the chorus.

Chorus

> Instead of spa we'll drink down ale,
> And pay the reck'ning on the nail;
> No man for debt shall go to gaol
>   From Garry Owen in glory.

Custer was nearly as often in the midst of trouble as he was in the thick of the fighting, for he, a stern disciplinarian to his men, had a contradictory streak of insubordination toward his superiors, and his career was spotted with controversies and courts-martial. It was he who had shot and hanged five of Mosby's Rangers during the Civil War, with consequent retaliation upon his own men. The volunteer Michigan cavalry regiment which he had led to Texas had virtually mutinied because the men wanted to go home and not to the frontier, and Custer's discipline on these unwilling men was curt and harsh. Later, after he joined the 7th Cavalry in Kansas, he had ordered his officers, in pursuit of deserters, "to bring in none alive." Soon afterwards, he was court-martialed himself for deserting his command to ride to his wife's side, and was "suspended from rank and command for one year" in September, 1867.

Custer joined the newly born 7th Cavalry at Fort Riley, Kansas, in September, 1866. From the start it was an unusual regiment. The officers and men were an experienced if heterogeneous lot and it contained many colorful soldiers of fortune. Among the officers there were only three West Pointers, including the absent Colonel Andrew J. Smith, Custer himself, and one major. The other officers included a Frenchman, a Prussian, a former member of Congress, a half-breed Indian, an ex-judge, a former papal Zouave, and a grandson of Alexander Hamilton.

In the spring of 1867, General Winfield Scott Hancock, later to run as the Democratic nominee for the presidency in 1880, led out a column, including four companies of the 7th under Custer, to punish the rampaging Indians. He accomplished little except a few futile parleys which frightened the Indians into dispersing all over the wide prairies and making more trouble in detail. It was during this expedition that Custer set such a killing pace that his men deserted in droves and he issued the order to shoot them on sight. Also during this trek, Lieutenant Kidder of the 2nd Cavalry, with ten of his men and a Sioux guide, bearing dispatches to Custer, were killed and frightfully mutilated by the Indians. Custer and his column ran across the remains of this detachment and his description, as given in his book *My Life on the Plains,* is a fair sample of what the Indians did to their defeated foes:

Every individual of the party had been scalped and his skull broken. . . .

Even the clothes of all the party had been carried away; some of the bodies were lying in beds of ashes, with partly burned

George A. Custer, My Life on the Plains.
Harvard College Library

Custer finding the remains of Lieutenant Kidder and his men

fragments of wood near them, showing that the savages had put some of them to death by the terrible tortures of fire. The sinews of the arms and legs had been cut away, the nose of every man hacked off, and the features otherwise defaced so that it would have been scarcely possible for even a relative to recognize a single one of the unfortunate victims. We could not even distinguish the officer from his men. Each body was pierced by from twenty to fifty arrows, and the arrows were found as the savage demons had left them, bristling in the bodies.

Perhaps this sort of thing, which was common enough after an Indian victory, was what impelled General Phil Sheridan to say "The only good Indian is a dead Indian."

The next year, in 1868, Sheridan, who had assumed command in the West, decided that the way to corner and defeat the elusive and destructive Indians was to attack them in their winter camps where they were concentrated, snugly holed up, and immobile, a tactic which had never before been tried because of the severity of the winters on the Great Plains. So the 7th Cavalry under Custer, who had been called back to duty from his suspension by his good friend and old commanding officer Sheridan, rode out into the November cold from Camp Supply, in what is now northwestern Oklahoma, into a blizzard in which the temperature dropped to seven below zero. Riding south, they forded the icy Canadian River and that night their Indian scouts reported a large Indian village on the banks of the Washita River. This proved to belong to the Cheyennes under Black Kettle who had succeeded Roman Nose, killed in the assault on the island defended by Forsyth and his men the previous September.

Custer divided the regiment into four attack groups which surrounded the sleeping village and waited silently for four

George A. Custer, My Life on the Plains.
Harvard College Library

*Custer's dawn attack on Black Kettle's camp on
the Washita River, November, 1868*

hours in the bitter cold. At daybreak, the regimental band, as a
signal for attack, crashed into "Garry Owen," and the troopers
charged into the village. It was soon over. The Cheyennes were
completely surprised and 103 warriors killed and fifty-three
squaws and children captured. During the height of the fighting
Major Elliott, leading nineteen troopers, dashed after a band
of fugitive Indians and was lost to sight. Soon large numbers of
Indians were noticed on the bluffs below the destroyed village
and reports came in that there were other villages and many Indians farther down the river who were massing for a counter-
attack.

164

Custer knew he must retreat to join his main supply train, moving toward him, miles behind, before the Indians discovered and destroyed it. He ordered the destruction of the village lodges and their contents and the shooting of seven hundred captured ponies, placed the captured women and children in the ammunition wagons, and with the band playing "Ain't I Glad to Get Out of the Wilderness," he headed the column straight down the valley toward the other villages in a bold effort to outface the threatening Indians and to find Major Elliott and his men. But the search was in vain. No signs of the missing detachment were found. Elliott and his men had been cut off and all killed by the overwhelming numbers of Cheyennes, Kiowas, Comanches, and Apaches who lived in this communal winter camp. The 7th rode on till darkness when Custer suddenly faced it about to avoid an ambush and led it safely back to report to General Sheridan at Camp Supply, which it entered triumphantly to the tune of "Garry Owen." Besides Elliott and his men, Captain Louis McLane Hamilton, the grandson of Alexander Hamilton, had been killed, and a few men wounded. The next month, Custer returned to the field of battle with General Sheridan and found the mutilated bodies of Elliott and his men.

After the Battle of the Washita, the untiring Custer led his regiment on many long and grueling marches over the prairies, with the band often lifting the flagging morale of his tired troopers. And Custer's exuberant vitality was almost supernatural. Often he would spend a long day of fourteen hours in the saddle and then pass the greater part of the night talking and skylarking with his family or friends, or writing at his desk. He was devoted to his attractive wife and when in the field never failed to write her each night a many-paged letter which might not be finished until daybreak. Then, after a rest of an hour or so, he would leap into the saddle and lead the column on another killing ride which left his officers and men staggering from fatigue. And Custer could keep this up day after day to the mortification of many younger but exhausted officers and men. On one of these marches, he went alone into the lodge of a band of Cheyennes and obtained the release of two captive white girls by a swap of three Indian prisoners — a most diplomatic and courageous accomplishment considering the bad feeling on both sides. Peace now reigned for a while on the plains and the 7th Cavalry relaxed to hunt, dance, and enjoy garrison life. In 1871, the regiment moved to the South for occupation duty and Custer found time to write a series of articles which were published in 1875 as *My Life on the Plains*.

In 1873, the 7th Cavalry returned to the frontier, to a camp near Yankton, South Dakota; and in June, Custer led ten companies of the regiment, as part of an expedition, to survey a railroad route up the Yellowstone River during which march he had several brushes with the hostile Sioux. The next year he explored the Black Hills, which had been recognized as Sioux territory by treaty, and enthusiastically reported the discovery of rich deposits of gold. This news appeared in newspaper headlines all over the country and a gold rush began which soon trampled on all agreements protecting the Sioux's claim to this area. The result was that many of that aggrieved tribe, joined by the Cheyennes, went off the reservation and on to the war path in the spring of 1876.

In May of that year, Custer led out his regiment, some six hundred men, armed with carbines and revolvers, from Fort Abraham Lincoln, across the Missouri River from Bismarck, North Dakota, on his last ride. He was smarting from a sharp reprimand from President Grant and General Sherman for just previously offering some unsubstantiated and hearsay evidence to a Congressional committee investigating Indian affairs, which had reflected on Grant's brother. He had been relieved of his command in consequence and only his frantic pleas to General Sheridan had brought about his reinstatement. Custer was doubtless determined to redeem himself at all costs, and to a man of his temperament this meant the taking of long and reckless chances.

The 7th Cavalry formed part of a column, commanded by General Alfred Terry, which was to co-operate with two other columns, one led by General George Crook, and the other by Colonel John Gibbon. All three were to converge on the rebellious Sioux and Cheyennes who were somewhere south of the Yellowstone River in Montana. Before this plan could be effected Chief Crazy Horse of the Sioux repulsed Crook's force, which was advancing from the south, near the Rosebud River, and forced it to retreat.

And this brings us to that matchless leader and unconquerable Sioux warrior, Crazy Horse, who was the military genius of the mounted Sioux nation. Unfortunately no unquestionably authentic picture of him seems to exist, and especially so as General Miles described him as the "personification of savage ferocity." General Crook, who had been one of Sheridan's cavalry commanders during the Civil War and whom we shall meet again in the next chapter, had been brought north from Arizona for the campaign against the Sioux. He had led out a force of ten companies of cavalry and two of infantry from Fort Fetterman in Wyoming in March and had run across a Sioux trail. He sent six troops of cavalry under Colonel Reynolds to follow this, and they stumbled upon a hidden Sioux village which they captured

*Crazy Horse's Sioux warriors charging General Crook's
column at the Rosebud River, Montana, June 17, 1876*

by a surprise attack and destroyed, although most of the Indians
escaped.* But the chief of this village was the bold and skillful
Crazy Horse. Rallying his fleeing men he fell like a nest of
frantic hornets on the attackers, who probably outnumbered his

* "In describing the village and its furnishings the historian of the Crook
expedition tells us that it was bountifully provided with all the luxuries that a
savage could desire, and much that a white man would not disdain to class
among the substantial comforts of civilized life." P. E. Byrne, *Soldiers of the
Plains* (New York, 1926).

168

warriors by a half and who were infinitely better equipped in every way, especially in clothing, because the Sioux had fled their teepees in the freezing temperature with little besides their weapons. Crazy Horse by his superb and inspiring leadership led his men back again and again to harass the troopers with hit-and-run attacks and finally achieved the incredible by driving them from the field. Later, after Reynolds had rejoined Crook, the Indians recaptured many of their horses and even made away with the command's herd of beef cattle. The result of this reversal was that Crook and his meatless men had to return to their base and start all over again. It was one of those rare occasions when the hackneyed phrase about "snatching victory from the jaws of defeat" literally applied; and it has been called a more spectacular feat than Phil Sheridan's leading the routed Federals back to victory at Cedar Creek after his ride from Winchester (1864), which many consider the greatest individual deed of the Civil War. The undaunted Crazy Horse deserved infinite credit for this near military-miracle.

The failure of this expedition was what decided the military planners to proceed on a larger scale and to send the three columns, mentioned above, after the defiant and formidable enemy. Following this plan, Crook started out again in May and once more met Crazy Horse and his warriors on the Rosebud River in Montana on June 17. Crazy Horse again led his braves into another epic battle, full of swift action, charges and counter-charges, with many separate melees swirling over ridges, in ravines, and on the plains. The numbers were about equal. Crook claimed the victory because he held the field of combat, but if so it was a Pyrrhic one. He was stopped cold and for the second time was forced to return to his supply base, and the triumphant Crazy Horse led his men on to join the big camp of the other Sioux and Cheyennes on the Little Big Horn River. This repulse was the key fight which prevented the co-operation of Crook and led to the Custer disaster eight days later.

However, Gibbon and Terry, who knew nothing of Crook's recent setback, met at the confluence of the Rosebud and Yellowstone Rivers and agreed upon a plan whereby Custer was to follow an Indian trail which had been discovered leading west to the Big Horn Mountains and then to wait at a point on the Little Big Horn River for the rest of the forces for a concerted attack. It was assumed that Crook was advancing from the south.

Custer led out the 7th, as always a thrilling sight, with whipping flags and guidons, and with trumpeters blowing in place of the band which had been left in garrison. A forced night march brought the regiment to the divide between the Rosebud and Little Big Horn Rivers, both of which flowed north into the Yellowstone River. At dawn of June 25, his scouts told Custer there were many Indians ahead, toward the Little Big Horn River to the west. In fact, there may have been 8000 to 10,000 Sioux and Cheyennes, with possibly 2500 to 3500 warriors under Chiefs Gall, Sitting Bull, and Crazy Horse, who was fresh from his victory over Crook. Custer's scouts also told him that Indians had been seen in his rear, which meant that his presence was known to the enemy. His forced march had brought him to the rendezvous ahead of schedule and now it meant that he must let the Indians escape or fight alone against an unknown force. Custer had never avoided a fight and, probably spurred on by a burning desire to erase his recent humiliation, he immediately prepared to attack the Indians alone.

Custer led the regiment on to the west and when about twelve miles from the river he detached a squadron, three companies,

CUSTER'S FIGHT
Drawn by WHITE BIRD
Northern Cheyenne Indian and
Warrior of Custer's Massacre
GIFT OF
Captain Richard L. Livermore
U. S. Army, retired.
U. S. M. A. Class of 1891

An Indian artist's picture of the Custer massacre by one who was present. Some of Custer's men are shown dismounted with their horses stampeding.

U.S. Military Academy Museum

under Captain Benteen and sent them off to the left, to the south, to scout for Indian signs in that direction; for until something was known of the enemy encampment and the number of hostiles, Custer was groping without a definite plan. He then sent Major Reno with another three companies, to the left, across a small tributary of the Little Big Horn River, later called Reno Creek, to ride closely parallel with his own column of five companies, all still riding toward the west. One company was sent to the rear to guard the lagging and heavily burdened pack train which carried the ammunition. About nine miles later Custer signaled Reno to recross the creek with his command, and the two columns rode side by side until they reached

171

a lone teepee containing a dead Indian with surrounding traces of an abandoned village. The scouts also sighted a band of forty Indians fleeing toward the Little Big Horn River which was still three miles distant. Then word came in that the Indian encampment lay ahead across the Little Big Horn River.

At this point, Custer ordered Reno to ford the Little Big Horn River and to charge the Indian village when seen, promising him close support. Reno then went on at a sharp trot. Custer followed for a time, less than a mile behind, and then obliqued off to the right and was lost to sight. It was the same tactic of dividing his force which he had used so successfully in the dawn attack on the Washita, but this time the Indians knew of his presence and were ready in strength.

Reno forded the river, formed his squadron into line, and galloped for about two and a half miles toward the Indian village which appeared to the north. Mounted Indians poured from the village and awaited his advance, circling about, kicking up much dust, and apparently in great numbers. Reno looked around for the promised help but could see no signs of Custer or Benteen. He halted, dismounted his men, and took shelter in a small patch of timber. At that time he had lost only one man and was not over six hundred yards from the village. The Indians began to fire at his detachment from all sides and Reno decided to retreat back across the river. He gave orders to mount, not by trumpet call, which could have been heard by all above the din and excitement, but by passing the word around; but this did not reach nearly a score of men who were left behind, some of whom later managed to rejoin him. Those that heard the command remounted and dashed desperately off, disorderly and unorganized, in a sort of panic flight led by Reno; and the Indians picked off the frantic troopers, right and left, as they leaped their horses pell-mell from a five-foot bank into the river and then scrambled up an equally steep opposite bank, to find shelter on top of a small wooded hill. By this time, three officers and twenty-nine troopers had been killed, seven wounded, and fifteen were missing, out of Reno's original strength of 112 — a casualty list of nearly fifty per cent. Reno's retreat released the bulk of the Indians from defending their village against him and allowed them to mass against Custer, who was approaching from another angle.

In the meantime, Custer and his five troops had ridden steadily ahead and away to the right from the other two detachments. Climbing a hill, Custer at last saw part of the Indian village, a few hundred tepees, ahead and to the left, across the river. A mile farther on he sent two messengers racing back and over to Benteen, one of them a trumpeter carrying a scribbled message: "Benteen. Come on. Big village. Be quick. Bring packs. P. S. Bring pac's."

Headline, New York Times, *July 6, 1876*

New York Times, *July 6, 1876*

MASSACRE OF OUR TROOPS.

FIVE COMPANIES KILLED BY INDIANS.

GEN. CUSTER AND SEVENTEEN COMMISSIONED OFFICERS BUTCHERED IN A BATTLE ON THE LITTLE HORN—ATTACK ON AN OVERWHELMINGLY LARGE CAMP OF SAVAGES—THREE HUNDRED AND FIFTEEN MEN KILLED AND THIRTY-ONE WOUNDED—TWO BROTHERS, TWO NEPHEWS, AND A BROTHER-IN-LAW OF CUSTER AMONG THE KILLED—THE BATTLE-FIELD LIKE A SLAUGHTER-PEN.

SALT LAKE, July 5.—The special correspondent of the Helena (Montana) *Herald* writes from Stillwater, Montana, under date of July 2, as follows:

Muggins Taylor, a scout for Gen. Gibbon, arrived here last night direct from Little Horn River, and reports that Gen. Custer found the Indian camp of 2,000 lodges on the Little Horn, and immediately attacked it. He charged the thickest portion of the camp with five companies. Nothing is known of the operations of this detachment, except their course as traced by the dead. Major Reno commanded the other seven companies, and attacked the lower portion of the camp. The Indians poured a murderous fire from all directions. Gen. Custer, his two brothers, his nephew, and brother-in-law were all killed, and not one of his detachment escaped. Two hundred and seven men were buried in one place. The number of killed is estimated at 300, and the wounded at thirty-one.

The Indians surrounded Major Reno's command and held them one day in the hills cut off from water, until Gibbon's command came in sight, when they broke camp in the night and left. The Seventh fought like tigers, and were overcome by mere brute force.

The Indian loss cannot be estimated as they bore off and cached most of their killed. The remnant of the Seventh Cavalry and Gibbon's command are returning to the mouth of the Little Horn, where a steam-boat lies. The Indians got all the arms of the killed soldiers. There were seventeen commissioned officers killed. The whole Custer family died at the head of their column.

The exact loss is not known as both Adjutants and the Sergeant-major were killed. The Indian camp was from three to four miles long, and was twenty miles up the Little Horn from its mouth.

The Indians actually pulled men off their horses, in some instances.

This report is given as Taylor told it, as he was over the field after the battle. The above is confirmed by other letters, which say Custer has met with a fearful disaster.

Benteen, who had been scouting for miles without seeing an Indian, had turned back toward Custer's route when he received this message. He continued at a trot until he came to Reno's command in its new position where he stopped to help, although most of the enemy had left that area to attack Custer. There was no sign of Custer anywhere in view. The pack train straggled in behind Benteen during the next hour. Benteen's reinforcement and the ammunition probably saved Reno's command from later annihilation, but for the time being all was comparatively quiet.

Then came the sound of violently heavy firing up the river valley toward the Indian village. Custer was in action. After much delay, Captain Weir of Benteen's squadron, incensed that no help was being sent to Custer, led his troops forward about a mile; and after more hesitation and argument, Reno, as senior officer, finally gave the order for all to move to Custer's assistance. This was difficult to obey. The wounded had to be carried with the column, stretched on blankets which were held by the edges by mounted troopers, and this slowed the pace to a walk. Before they had moved more than a short way, it was too late. Custer's force had been wiped out although the men of the surviving squadrons did not realize it. But a tidal wave of screeching, exultant braves, returning from the massacre, pushed the little column back to the hill. For the rest of that day, they fought for their lives with a loss of eighteen killed and forty-three wounded. All through the hideous night the fight went on, to a horrible background of scalp dances in the valley below and the sounds of trumpet calls blown on captured bugles. All through the next morning the Indians attacked and were hurled back. Benteen was a pillar of strength in the defense and led the countercharges which threw back the endless waves of savages.

There were other deeds of heroism which won Medals of Honor: Sergeant Hanley galloped out and led back a stampeding mule carrying ammunition, which had run away among the Indians; others dashed through the enemy fire to fill canteens with water from the river for their comrades. Suddenly in the afternoon the Indian attacks ceased, and the worn-out defenders waited and watched for relief, hoping that Custer, whose fate they did not know, or Terry's oncoming column would appear before the Indians returned.

What had happened to Custer during this confusion? Nobody will ever really know and the guesses are contradictory. He evidently rode forward, behind a ridge on the east side of the river, until he sighted the village. The returning messengers last saw him and his men galloping down a ravine toward the river. He was probably soon slowed down by furious mounted flank attacks led by Chiefs Gall, Crazy Horse, and Rain-in-the-Face at the head of the frenzied Sioux and Cheyennes. His front was blocked as well and the column must have dismounted to defend itself. That probably sealed its doom. The horses were stampeded or killed and the men marooned on foot. The Indians were well armed with repeating rifles of greater range than the cavalry carbines and plentifully supplied with ammunition, some of which had been captured during the repulse of General Crook's force a week before. There is evidence that the Indians did great damage with clouds of arrows, which they fired from surrounding concealed gullies in an arc. Probably, and despite the imaginative illustrations of the battle, there were no heavy mounted charges by the Indians until the very end. They were not necessary. Custer's men only had one hundred rounds of ammunition apiece, and when this was gone they were helpless. The Indians, in overwhelming numbers, probably soon

175

*Rain-in-the-Face, whom Long-
fellow versified as killing Custer*

melted away the surrounded and exposed group with rifle fire
and arrows until none were left. Nobody knows or ever will
know exactly what happened. Strangely enough, Custer's body
was unmutilated and the Indians probably did not know who
he was. Despite this fact, the rumor grew and persisted that
Rain-in-the-Face had cut out Custer's heart; and Longfellow
dignified this myth in his poem "The Revenge of Rain-in-the-
Face," one stanza of which read:

> But the foemen fled in the night,
> And Rain-in-the-Face, in his flight,
>   Uplifted high in air
>   As a ghastly trophy, bore
>   The brave heart, that beat no more,
> Of the White Chief with yellow hair.

The only survivor of the carnage was Captain Keogh's horse "Comanche," who was found wounded on the field by Terry's relief column and tenderly nursed back to health. "Comanche" was never again ridden or worked; in all parades of the 7th he was led, bridled and saddled, by a trooper. On paydays the soldiers brought him buckets of beer and he lived on until 1891, the most privileged member of the regiment.

National Archives

The only survivor, Comanche, Captain Keogh's horse, who lived on till 1891 as the most privileged member of the Seventh Cavalry

On the second day after Custer's death, Terry and Gibbon arrived on the scene with their columns. They first relieved Reno's and Benteen's entrenched survivors, and then buried all the dead on both battlefields and cared for the wounded as best they could. Captain Benteen walked about the site of his commanding officer's last stand; and his remarks about it, at a Court of Inquiry, were firsthand and the opinion of a brave and experienced officer who knew what he was talking about. Benteen gave his reasons for the defeat, and time does not seem to have produced any better ones:

> There were a great deal too many Indians who were powerful good shots on the other side. We were at their hearths and homes — and they were fighting for all the good God gives anyone to fight for.

The total loss of the 7th Cavalry in the battle was: Custer and 212 of his men, all killed; of Benteen's and Reno's commands, sixty-four men killed and fifty-one wounded; a total casualty list of over half the regiment of six hundred men. The Indian losses were probably comparatively low. Rarely have trained troops been so defeated by savages. Custer unquestionably made the mistake of underestimating the Indians' prowess and numbers and of launching a divided attack without a proper reconnaissance. But the blame must be shared by his higher command who also underguessed the strength of the enemy. Certainly General Terry should not have originally divided his forces to corral the Indians, who were at least twice as strong as the force which, under Crazy Horse, had repulsed Crook at the Rosebud River. And Crook's force had been as strong as the combined forces of Terry, Gibbon, and Custer. Whatever may be said of Custer, he was a soldier of great distinction and went to his death as a soldier should, unafraid and facing the blows of an intrepid foe.

After the Custer defeat, General Sheridan stripped every post of its men from the line of Canada to Mexico and poured these troops into the Sioux country. General Crook had command of the field operations, and Colonel Ranald Slidell Mackenzie of the 4th Cavalry, who had come up from Texas, crushed the Cheyennes in November, as we shall see later. Sitting Bull and his followers fled over the border to Canada, and the remaining Sioux gradually surrendered; but Sheridan said he did not consider the war with the great Sioux nation, the most powerful and warlike of all the Indian tribes, to be over until September, 1877. The Sioux were born horsemen — perhaps the finest light cavalry the world has ever seen — and inflicted the heaviest losses which our army received during all our Indian wars.

"Mounted Indian," by Frederic Remington

CHAPTER VIII

Trouble with the Lesser Tribes
1865 – 1890

No sooner had the Sioux war ended than another began
under the leadership of an Indian chief who rivaled Crazy
Horse as a born military genius, a sort of natural Napoleon —
Chief Joseph of the Lower Nez Percé Indians (the early French
traders gave these people the name Pierced Noses). Nothing
has ever surpassed the retreat of this tribe from eastern Idaho
to northern Montana, in 1877, under this extraordinary man.
It has been compared, with good reason, to the march of Xeno-
phon and the ten thousand Greeks. This tribe had always had
friendly relations with the whites since the appearance of Lewis
and Clark in the Northwest in 1806; in fact they boasted they
had never killed a white man; but, because of some underhanded skulduggery by the Indian agents of the Interior Department, they were deprived of the lands of their forefathers.
The army, as usual, had to do the dirty work of moving these
rightfully indignant Indians to an undesired reservation. To enforce the order, in June 1877, two companies of the 1st Cavalry
and some mounted civilians were sent to White Bird Canyon in
Idaho where the rebellious tribe had gathered. Chief Joseph,
who had had no previous experience whatever in warfare, skill-
fully ambushed this command and sent it reeling back with a
loss of one third its number, sixty-nine men killed, which next to

the Custer disaster was the most crushing defeat ever inflicted by the Indians. The victory was won by Chief Joseph with half his warriors armed only with bows and arrows; and none of them had had any experience in war.

My Bunky and Others. *Library of Congress*

"The Lost Dispatches" by Charles Schreyvogel

This of course opened the floodgates, and a sizable mixed column, with some five hundred cavalry and a small detachment of artillery, was collected and hurried forward under the command of General O. O. Howard of Maine, a one-armed veteran of the Civil War. Chief Joseph in the meantime had moved to a stronger position on the Clearwater River where, with an inferior force, he calmly awaited the approach of this well-equipped punitive expedition. On July 11, these forces met, and about three hundred untrained Indians not only fought nearly six hundred regular soldiers to a standstill in hand-to-hand fighting but captured, for a while, all of Howard's artillery in a cavalry charge. Joseph and his band then began their retreat toward the Canadian border, in which country Sitting Bull and his braves had found refuge after the Custer massacre.

This was too much, and the telegraph wires buzzed with orders converging all available troops, even from as far away as Georgia, onto the path of Joseph's obvious retreat. Attack after attack gradually decimated the small band but still Joseph fought back with masterful skill, inflicting heavy losses on his pursuers, and kept on his way. At one point in this anabasis, Joseph declared he was tired of being trailed and, forming some fifty of his mounted braves into a precise column of fours, rode at night, past a sentry who believed it to be a returning detachment of cavalry, into the heart of Howard's camp, which his men then proceeded to shoot up in glorious style and to stampede Howard's vital pack train. To cap this, he laid an ambush for the pursuing troopers and shot them up as well; and all this without the loss of a man. It was most humiliating to Howard who was forced to fall back in the chase.

Pushing on, Joseph began to meet what must have seemed like the whole United States Army, frantically summoned to block

"The Truce." Surrender of Chief Joseph, by Frederic Remington

his small band, by then only about one hundred warriors. The 5th Cavalry appeared from southern Montana, and Colonel Nelson A. Miles arrived with a mixed detachment which included five troops of the 2nd and 7th Cavalry. This overwhelming force fell on the remnants of Joseph's tribe, who were within forty miles of the Canadian border, but, after severe fighting at close quarters, was repulsed. For four days Joseph held out against these odds and then, at last, gave in. The tribe had only 87 surviving warriors, 40 of them wounded; 184 squaws and 147 children, many wounded; and all badly weakened by starvation. His dignified words of surrender epitomized the tragedy of the American Indian:

> Tell General Howard that I know his heart. . . . I am tired of fighting. Our chiefs are killed. . . . It is cold and we have no blankets. The little children are freezing to death. My people — some of them — have run away to the hills, and we have no blankets, no food. No one knows where they are — perhaps freezing to death. I want to have time to look for my children, and to see how many of them I can find; maybe I shall find them among the dead. Hear me, my chiefs, my heart is sick and sad. From where the sun now stands, I will fight no more forever.

Nowadays, the people of what was once the frontier like to boast, in retrospect, about how bad and tough were the Indians who once plagued their particular area. The Texans, for example, claim that the Comanches were better horsemen, fiercer and abler warriors, and committed greater damages than the more famous Sioux tribes to the north. This was the same tribe which George Catlin had met and sketched, way back in 1834, while accompanying Colonel Henry Dodge and the old 1st Dragoons on a friendly visit to the frontier tribes. The question of which tribe was more destructive is debatable. Both were tops in mounted warfare. Certainly the Sioux were more numerous but the Comanches had been fighting the Mexicans for years before the arrival of the Americans and then had turned their full hostilities against the Texans long before the Sioux took up arms against the encroaching white men, so that the sum total of their depredations may well have been greater.

The Comanche raids into Mexico were fabulous and like unto those of Attila and the Huns which laid completely waste a countryside and earned the title of the "scourge of God." Like the untamed Apaches to the west, the Comanches had never been conquered by the Spaniards and for years devastated northern Mexico on an even larger scale than the Apaches. From their range in the Staked Plains of West Texas they annually swooped down in force on the Mexican states of Chihuahua and Coahuila during the full moon of September. Riding half-wild horses, on stirrupless pads of buffalo hide, armed with lances of ash, and carrying shields of buffalo bull hides which could deflect a bullet, they, the finest horsemen of all the Indian tribes, poured down a marked trail, worn deep by their incursions and lined for five hundred miles with horses' bones, and then scattered to plunder, kill, and to capture children to be brought up in the tribe, young women for squaws, and many, many horses. The Mexicans were so terrorized that they seldom offered organized resistance, although the raids were made regularly at the same time of year, and resignedly accepted these annual forays during "the moon of the Comanches." This fierce and turbulent tribe had become bitterly hostile to the Texans and turned much of their warlike energies against them, and harassed the frontier settlements in a crescendo during the distractions of the Civil War.

In fact, Texas was probably in worse shape from Indian depredations after the war than any other section of the country. The Southern Cheyennes and Arapahoes roamed over northern Texas while the Comanches, with their close allies the Kiowas, the Kickapoos, the Lipans, and the Mescalero Apaches, actually controlled western Texas and eastern New Mexico and ravaged freely back and forth from southern Colorado to the Rio Grande.

The Cheyennes and Arapahoes, when pursued, retreated to their reservations in the Indian Territory, the Comanches and the Kiowas had hidden retreats in the Staked Plains, south of the Canadian River, and the Kickapoos, Apaches, and Lipans hid over the border in Mexico. From these bases they all constantly prowled about the frontier settlements, stealing livestock, and attacking any settlers they met if the odds were in their favor. Texas got it from three sides.

The man who was sent to clean up this truly acute mess had been one of Sheridan's boy cavalry generals, Ranald Slidell Mackenzie, of whom Grant wrote in his *Memoirs*, "I regarded Mackenzie as the most promising young officer in the Army." During the Civil War he had been wounded six times and at the end had risen to the rank of major general in command of a cavalry corps — all in less than three years of service and before his twenty-fifth birthday.

Mackenzie came from unusual stock. His father was Commodore Alexander Slidell Mackenzie of the navy, who was the center of a national controversy after he hanged Midshipman John Spencer of New York to the yardarm of his ship for mutiny, without a trial, in 1842. Spencer only happened to be the son of the Secretary of War and the repercussions can be imagined. Herman Melville is believed to have used the incident for the plot of his *Billy Budd*. The commodore was also an author whose excellent book, now forgotten, *A Year in Spain,* strongly influenced the writings about Spain of his intimate friend Washington Irving. Ranald Mackenzie's uncle was John Slidell, the Confederate Commissioner to France, of the Mason-Slidell incident, which nearly involved the United States in war with Great Britain in 1861. His aunt married Commodore Matthew C. Perry, who opened up Japan to the western world in 1853, and their daughter married August Belmont of New York. His younger brother, a lieutenant commander in the navy, was killed in 1867 while leading a charge against the savages of the island of Formosa. They were an impetuous and daring breed and Ranald led the tribe.

Born in New York, young Mackenzie attended Williams College for three years and then entered West Point, where he graduated in 1862 at the head of his class. After about two years of exceptional service with the Engineers, he was appointed the colonel of the Second Connecticut Volunteers, Heavy Artillery but acting as infantry. Mackenzie replaced a hard-boiled colonel who had been killed, but dealt in scorpions where his predecessor had chastened with whips in enforcing discipline, and he became a greater terror to the officers and men than rebel grape and canister. Before the Shenandoah campaign in the autumn of 1864, there was a regimental tradition of a well-defined purpose to dispose of him in the next battle. But at the Battle of Winchester in September, the rumored plot of the men quailed and failed before his audacious courage. He galloped up and down the front of his men, with his hat on his saber, through a hailstorm of lead, and nobody could take a shot at so brave a man. His horse was cut in two by a shell and he was seriously wounded but refused to leave the field. A month later, at Cedar Creek, he was wounded twice more and this time was forced to give up command of the regiment, which by that time had completely changed its opinions and swore by him. In December he was back in action, as a brigadier general in command of a division, and he rose to be a major general, one of Sheridan's young cavalry tigers, in command of a cavalry corps at Five Forks and during the final actions with Lee's army.

Ranald S. Mackenzie as a brigadier-general of volunteers
during the Civil War. He was twenty-four years old.

Mackenzie, as a twenty-four-year-old major general, was a spare, slim young man of medium height and frail physique. His youth was accentuated by his being clean-shaven, in a day of heavily bearded men, except for long sideburns to the curve of his jaws. He had an ascetic, hawklike face and looked a bit as Ralph Waldo Emerson might have, if that philosopher had been exposed to shot and shell instead of transcendentalism.

After the war, Mackenzie had filled various assignments, mostly on the Texas frontier, until he was appointed colonel of the 4th Cavalry in 1871 — the old 1st Cavalry, which had been the regiment of Edwin Vose Sumner, George B. McClellan, Joseph E. Johnston, and Jeb Stuart.

Mackenzie decided the only way to stop the murderous Indian forays against the Texas settlements was to destroy the Indian bases and so, in the summer and fall of 1871, he began a series of whirlwind campaigns which accomplished this within three years. First, he smashed into the Staked Plains in West Texas, an area almost completely unknown to the white man, and flushed out Chief Quanah Parker, the famous half-breed Comanche chief, and his followers. During this expedition, the colonel was shot in the leg by an arrow, his seventh wound.

Quanah Parker was an unusual leader. His father had been a Kwadahi chief, the most hostile and turbulent branch of the tribe, and his mother was a white girl, Cynthia Ann Parker, who had been captured at a massacre of Texas settlers in 1836, nine years before Quanah's birth. In 1866 he organized his own band and terrorized the Texas frontier for the next nine years until he finally surrendered to Ranald Mackenzie in 1875. Unlike many other subdued Indians, he quickly took to civilization and became popular among his former enemies as a noted raconteur of highly improper stories. He capped his reformation by riding in state at the inaugural parade for President Theodore Roosevelt in March, 1905.

In 1872, Mackenzie pursued a band of thieving Indians all the way across West Texas into New Mexico and, while unsuccessful in catching them, he gained immensely valuable experience and information about that unexplored country. That autumn he moved up into what is now Oklahoma and made a successful surprise attack on a large Comanche village near the

"The Last Drop," by Charles Schreyvogel

Quanah Parker, half-white chief of the Comanches, 1868

Red River, in which he captured a herd of 3000 horses. That night the surviving Comanches stampeded the herd and regained their horses plus others belonging to the troopers. After that painful lesson, Mackenzie always shot all captured horses.

In the meantime, while the indefatigable colonel was attacking the Comanches to the west and north, the tribes living in Mexico were lacerating the southern Texas frontier. These Indians kept on friendly terms with the Mexicans and after a bloody raid into Texas would scamper home where they were protected by international law from reprisals. There was a strong suspicion that the Mexican authorities, ever resentful of Texas's independence and the losses of the Mexican War, rather enjoyed the situation; certainly they refused to co-operate in ending it.

The matter became so acute that Secretary of War W. W. Belknap and General Phil Sheridan came to Fort Clark, Texas, in April, 1873, for a conference with Colonel Mackenzie, who had just arrived at that post with the 4th Cavalry. Captain R. G. Carter, of that regiment, wrote, years later, in his book *On the Border with Mackenzie,* that Sheridan told Mackenzie to enter Mexican territory and destroy a nest of raiding Lipans, Kickapoos, and Apaches at Remolina, a village about sixty miles south of the border. When Mackenzie asked for written orders to protect himself for this gross breach of Mexican sovereignty, Sheridan pounded the table and shouted:

Damn the orders! Damn the authority! You are to go ahead on your own plan of action and your authority and backing shall be General Grant [then President] and myself. With us behind you in whatever you do to clean up this situation, you can rest assured of the fullest support. You must assume the risk. We will assume the final responsibility should any result.

It was a difficult situation for the colonel. No force of United States troops had officially entered Mexico since the Mexican War. If he failed, the full blame would probably be his.

The next month, on May 17, Colonel Mackenzie moved out suddenly against the distant Indian village in Mexico. Leading a column of nearly four hundred men, he crossed the Rio Grande in the evening and headed southwest. All that night they rode steadily in clouds of dust, in a faint moonlight, at a trot or gallop, dropping their pack train after midnight to hasten their progress.

It was broad daylight when the Indian village was sighted. Mackenzie led his tired men in a hell-for-leather charge into its midst, taking the Indians completely by surprise. When the dust, shooting, powder smoke, and general furor finally settled and ceased, the dismounted troopers counted nineteen dead Lipan braves, and the chief and forty women and children as captives. The losses of the 4th Cavalry were one killed and two wounded. There was no time for rest and Mackenzie started at once upon the back track, with the captives tied on captured ponies.

The return was a nightmare. The hostile countryside had been aroused and closed in around the slow-moving column. The exhausted troopers reeled in their saddles from hunger and lack of sleep and the frightful heat of the sun bore down like a giant press. A haggard rearguard prodded stragglers, asleep on their horses, back into line and held off a threatened attack by hundreds of infuriated Mexicans who snowballed in numbers as the distance to the Rio Grande lessened. The river was finally reached in the morning and the column splashed through the shallows to safety, after riding 160 miles in thirty-two hours with no rest or food. Mackenzie had gambled and

Outing Magazine, *April 1887. Harvard College Library*

The return from Remolina, May, 1873. By Frederic Remington.

won; and the raids into Texas from that particular area stopped. There were, however, indignant protests from the Mexican government; in fact it looked for a while as if war might result. But Sheridan kept his word and Mackenzie suffered no disciplinary action. Later, the colonel, or his officers, crossed the river several times more, in pursuit of marauding Indians, until the border menace completely ceased.

The next year, in 1874, Colonel Mackenzie surprised a war party of several hundred Southern Cheyennes in a deep canyon in the Staked Plains, near what is now Amarillo, Texas, and captured a herd of 2000 horses — which, remembering his earlier experience of the stampede, he destroyed. This was a knockout blow to the Cheyennes and forced their return to the reservation and consequent good behavior. In the autumn Mackenzie and eight companies of the 4th Cavalry had another encounter with a wandering band of marauding Indians and killed two and captured nineteen.

After the destruction of Custer in June, 1876, Mackenzie was ordered north to act under General George Crook, who had been summoned from Arizona. In November, he led a column of 1500 cavalry and four hundred mounted Indian auxiliaries against Chief Dull Knife and his Northern Cheyennes who had been lurking near the Powder River in Wyoming since their defeat of Custer. This tribe was less numerous than the Sioux but they were more resolute and fiercer. Once again, Mackenzie made a surprise attack, after waiting until dawn in a canyon listening to the Indian war drums celebrating their recent victories. The camp and all its supplies were destroyed, about one hundred Indians killed, and six hundred ponies captured. Many of those who escaped later froze to death in a temperature of thirty degrees below zero. After this thorough beating, the Cheyennes soon surrendered and the troubles in the north ended.

Mackenzie's surprise attacks upon the Indians were always successful. There seems to be a belief that this kind of attack was an Indian specialty, but time and again Mackenzie crept up on the enemy and struck at dawn. Indians were inclined to stay-a-bed habits in their own camps and seemed to lack the organi-

"The Trooper." Cover drawing by Frederic Remington
used for years on the Cavalry Journal.

zation to post sentinels against a swift-striking foe. Mackenzie had learned this and used these tactics to his advantage.

After this victory, Mackenzie moved all over the Southwest as a sort of trouble shooter for difficult Indian and frontier situations. He crossed the border twice again in pursuit of raiding Indians but managed to avoid any hostilities with the outraged Mexican troops. This miserable border situation was finally settled when President Porfirio Diaz agreed to police the Mexican side, and a friendly agreement to co-operate was reached between General Geronimo Trevino of the Mexican army and his father-in-law, Major General Edward Otho Cresap Ord, in command of the Department of Texas. General Ord, incidentally, was a legitimate grandson of King George IV of England by his morganatic marriage to Mrs. Maria Smythe FitzHerbert — but that is all another, although fascinating, story.

Then Mackenzie twice went to Colorado and peacefully settled two extremely dangerous situations with the tribe of Utes who had killed their Indian agent and then had defeated a punitive column sent against them. On his second visit Mackenzie, unarmed, faced twenty armed and truculent chiefs and by his firmness made them agree to move to another reservation in Utah, an order which they had sworn to die fighting against before obeying. In 1881, he was in command of all forces in Arizona, with headquarters at Fort Apache, and kept complete peace and order in that turbulent territory. He then went to Santa Fe, New Mexico, where he was promoted to brigadier general.

Promotion was snail-slow in those days, and the competition was keen. Nelson A. Miles of the infantry had received the same promotion two years before, and there had been a keen rivalry between these two Indian-fighting colonels. There was an apocryphal tale of an old and privileged sergeant who had noticed Colonel Mackenzie, one night in a prairie camp, gazing thoughtfully at the heavens, and remarked, "Colonel, there's Miles between you and that star."

"Early Dawn Attack," by Charles Schreyvogel. This typifies one of Ranald Mackenzie's surprise attacks on an Indian village.

In the autumn of 1883, Mackenzie was placed in command of the Department of Texas, with headquarters at Fort Sam Houston in San Antonio. His frail physique and high-strung temperament had quite naturally been affected by his seven wounds and the hardships of years of campaigning in the field, and he was constantly racked by pain. His officers and men stepped lightly before him but always respected him for his innate modesty and courtesy and his unfailing courage. In San Antonio, General Mackenzie, who had remained a bachelor, met again the love of his life, a woman who had married another man but was now a widow, and their engagement soon followed. This sudden happiness seemed to have given an emotional fillip which, combined with the cumulative toll of his physical sufferings, unseated his reason. He was sent east to an asylum in December and was retired for disability in line of duty the following spring.

On the morning of January 20, 1889, the *New York Sunday Times* carried an account of the Yale Junior Promenade with the names of all the lovely young ladies who had attended that festivity. On other pages there were discussions of the prospects of the Harvard and Cornell crews for the coming rowing season and lists of the candidates reporting for practice. The rest of the paper bore foreign and domestic news of no startling importance. Tucked away in the obituary column a brief notice read:

> MACKENZIE — At New Brighton, Staten Island, on the 19th. January. Brig.-Gen. Ranald Slidell Mackenzie, United States Army, in the 48th year of his age.

This was all the death notice given to a man who ranked with Crook and Miles as an Indian fighter. The times were out of joint — not the man!

While all these troubles were going on in Texas and in the North, there was a distinct and peculiar war being waged against the venomous Apaches in Arizona and New Mexico, who were the most ferocious, the cruelest, and the craftiest of all the hostile Indians, and were aptly called by General Crook "the tigers of the human species." The Apache's hand had earlier been against the Spaniard and the Mexican and it was almost inevitably turned against the oncoming American. The Apaches excelled in the ambush and surprise attack, followed by the most shocking tortures and mutilations of those miserable unfortunates who were captured, which went far beyond the high average of the other Indians in their imaginative cruelty. Captives were slowly roasted alive, hanging head down over a fire; or the soles of their feet were sliced off and they were forced to walk on the broiling desert sand; or a prisoner might have his eyelids cut off and be staked on his back facing the sun, or next to an ant hill, or within reach of a tethered rattlesnake. Whatever it was, it was a slow death in agony which the fiendish Apaches considered the acme of good entertainment. The blazing sun of their country seemed to bake a deadly and malicious vitality and endurance into them which was embodied in their name *Apache* — the *Enemy*. They were the most elusive of foes and seemed to appear and disappear at will, clothed only in loincloths, leggings, and moccasins, with their straight black hair falling to their shoulders, bound back by a red strip of cloth around their foreheads. And almost always they could avoid mounted troops by their knowledge of the mountainous country and its inaccessible fastnesses and trails. General George Crook, whom Sherman called the greatest of our Indian fighters — and this opinion is quite generally accepted — found that only an Apache could catch an Apache,

201

John G. Bourke, *On the Border With Crook. Harvard College Library*

General George Crook, his mule, and two friendly Apaches

and by using their services as scouts against their brothers he was able to bring peace finally to a land drenched by the blood of centuries of warfare. These Apache Scouts were enrolled as a unit in the army and won great fame by their uncanny ability as trackers.

George Crook was an extraordinary man. Born near Dayton, Ohio, he graduated from West Point in 1852, and served as a lieutenant of infantry against the Indians on the Oregon frontier until he returned east to become colonel of an Ohio infantry regiment at the beginning of the Civil War. He soon became a brigadier general and, in command of a cavalry division, he defeated Joe Wheeler's Confederate cavalry in Tennessee in

202

1863. The next year, as a major general, he served in the Shenandoah Valley campaign, and afterwards commanded one of Sheridan's cavalry divisions during the last days of the war in the winter and early spring of 1865. He was a genial, kindly, and robust sixfooter who was distinguished by his bristly, flaring "Burnside" whiskers, only rivaled by those of Judson Kilpatrick. Dressed in canvas hunting clothes, he usually rode a mule on the march. He allowed his men a similar freedom of dress in the Arizona heat, and Captain Charles King of the 5th Cavalry, an officer who wrote several best-selling novels about life in the Old Army, described the astonishment of a newly arrived cavalry lieutenant from the East upon first beholding the garb of the men of his troop, which was part of Crook's command. The first sergeant wore an old gray-flannel shirt and a white Mexican sombrero, and his legs were encased in worn deerskin breeches; the men "had discarded pretty much every item of dress or equipment prescribed or furnished," for "Regardless of appearances or style himself, seeking only comfort in his dress, the chief [Crook] speedily found means to indicate that, in Apache-campaigning at least, it was — 'no red-tape when Indian-fighting.'"

Crook made a specialty of pack trains, almost to the point of a fetish, for he rightly judged that wheeled transport would be useless in any pursuit of the Apaches through and over the mountains, and he took pride in his nickname, "Granddaddy of the Pack Mules." By constant experiments and practice he brought the actual packing and the handling of the stubborn and unpredictable mules to a fine art. He even rode a mule himself, named "Apache," and his system of shaving the tails of new and unbroken mules as a warning to the unwary caused the army to apply the name "shavetail" to newly joined second lieu-

tenants who were still wet behind the ears. In his command for
the campaign against the Apaches in 1872 was the 5th Cavalry.

Arizona was a tough place in 1871 when Crook arrived to
take command. Many of the settlers were as fine a collection of
cutthroats and yeggs as could be found in all the wide-open
spaces of the Great West. They gave the Apaches a run for their
money in general lawlessness, and their atrocities often matched
the Indians' and aggravated the whole situation. But hardened
as they were, these settlers dreaded the Apaches, and, as an old
wagon-master remarked to a cavalry officer:

> We have a horror of them that you feel for a ghost. We never
> see them, but when on a road are always looking over our
> shoulders in anticipation. When they strike, all we see is the
> flash of the rifle resting with secure aim over a pile of stones,
> behind which, like a snake, the red murderer lies.*

Crook took his time in training his men and mules and made
one last effort to quiet the Apaches by conciliation but barely
escaped assassination by treachery at a conference. After that
things moved fast, and in late December, 1872, Major William
H. Brown with a battalion of the 5th Cavalry, guided by
friendly Apache scouts, cornered a strong body of hostiles in a
cave fortress in the Mazatal Mountains on the Salt River
Canyon. Brown led his dismounted troopers forward to surround
the cave, with author Lieutenant John Bourke in the forefront
of the action. It was like fighting a mad dog in a burrow. Finally
the troops poured over the stone barricade in front of the cave's
entrance and found seventy-four dead and wounded men,
women, and children in a sickening charnel house. Only eighteen were unhurt and made captive. The Apaches had refused

* Wesley Merritt, "Three Indian Campaigns," *Harper's New Monthly Magazine*, April, 1890.

"The Patient Pack-Mule," by Frederic Remington

an offer of safe conduct for their women and children and all had gone down fighting like wild beasts.

Crook gave the other recalcitrant Apaches no surcease from fighting but kept after them relentlessly day and night with his men and pack trains. Finally, in 1874, these human rattlesnakes of desert and mountain straggled back to their reservations. Crook treated them fairly and tried to put them on the road to peace and civilization by help and training in farming and grazing. But he was ordered north in 1875, after being promoted to brigadier general, where trouble was brewing among the Sioux and Cheyenne, and his constructive work was gradually undone by various crooked civilians of the Indian Bureau.

The notorious "Indian Ring" of politicians and traders battened off the hapless Apaches and lined their pockets with graft. Illegal whiskey-sellers prospered and the drunken Indians went back to their old habits and then once again murder and torture skulked along the desert trails of Arizona. Chiefs Victorio, Geronimo, and others would leave their reservations and lead small ravaging bands all along the border, darting back and forth across it, and leaving a train of horror behind them. Detachments of the colored 9th and 10th and the 3rd, 4th, and 6th Cavalry Regiments took up the pursuit but the wily chiefs would seek refuge in Mexico when hard pressed. Victorio was killed by Mexican troops in 1880, but Geronimo remained at large and added to his reputation as public enemy number one.

General Crook returned to Arizona in 1882 and by his ability and through the co-operation of the Mexican authorities, with whom an agreement was finally made which legalized the pursuit of the common enemy by our armed forces across the border, he pressed the errant Apaches hard. In the spring of 1883, Crook crossed into Mexico to attack a band of some five hundred Apaches lurking in the great Sierra Madre range under their chiefs Chato and Geronimo, and persuaded Geronimo to surrender his band and return to the reservation where Crook undertook to "set them to raising corn instead of scalps." This amenity lasted for almost three years and then in 1885, after a mammoth drunk on the reservation, Geronimo was off again, with a small band of followers, into the fastnesses of the Mexican mountains, with the 4th Cavalry in hot but unsuccessful pursuit.

Later that same year a small band of only eleven of Geronimo's warriors entered New Mexico in a raid which probably set a record for deviltry accomplished per man engaged. They traveled about 1200 miles, killed thirty-eight persons, captured and wore out 250 horses and mules, each man changing mounts at least twenty times, and finally escaped safely back over the border with the loss of but one man, although they were pursued, day and night, by five troops of cavalry. When a horse wore out, they killed it and removed its thirty to forty feet of small intestine, which they then cleaned, filled with water, and wrapped around a led horse. With this portable water supply, they shunned the valleys and water holes, which were all guarded, and moved only along the ridges at night, so that it was impossible for the pursuing cavalry to find or block them.

General Nelson A. Miles called Geronimo "the worst Indian who ever lived," and few questioned the title. He was a stocky, dark-faced man of about 170 pounds of muscle and sinew, who stood five feet eight inches, which was above the average Apache height. His face mirrored the cruelty and ferocity of his deeds; his eyes looked like bits of obsidian with a light behind them, and his mouth was a straight, thin-lipped gash in granite. The old cutthroat lived on until 1909, joined the Dutch Reformed Church, and made a very good thing out of selling his autographed photographs at the St. Louis World Fair in 1903 and at other gala affairs. He even rode with the Comanche chief, Quanah Parker, in a state coach at the inaugural parade for Theodore Roosevelt.

The next year, in January, 1886, at a spot two hundred miles south of the border, Captain Emmet Crawford, with a detachment of the 3rd Cavalry and some Apache scouts, cornered and badly defeated the old reprobate — whose name paratroopers now mispronounce as a shibboleth before leaping into space. But before Crawford could receive the Apache's surrender he himself was treacherously killed by Mexican irregular troops. Geronimo finally surrendered in April but that night a whiskey-seller sneaked into the Apache camp, and the next morning Geronimo and forty of his braves had disappeared — which meant the stale and weary chase must begin again.

At this time General Nelson A. Miles superseded Crook but kept closely to the same plans and followed Geronimo once more with 5000 men (the Apaches never numbered over eighty), among them detachments from several cavalry regiments based on Fort Huachuca or Fort Apache, which were the two main posts in Apache land. Miles introduced a communication novelty into the campaign in the heliostat, a portable mounted mirror, which by reflecting the sunlight could flash the dots and dashes of the Morse code for fifty miles or more. This had been used by the British army in India, and readers of Rudyard Kipling may remember his poem, "A Code of Morals," in which a young officer on the Afghan border, after teaching his new bride the code, flashed warnings to her at home, against the blandishments of "General Bangs — a most immoral man" — which were intercepted by the general and his staff, "dumb with pent-up mirth." The Apaches, however, were anything but mirthful about the efficiency of this new system of communication. In fact they were mystified by the swiftness with which Miles's scattered columns co-operated, and the new signaling device played an important part toward their final surrender.

Captain W. H. Lawton, of the 4th Cavalry, later to die as a general in the Philippines, and Surgeon Leonard Wood, afterwards colonel of the Rough Riders and Chief of Staff of the army, were the outstanding leaders in this new, and fortunately last, pursuit of the ghostlike Geronimo. Also along as a second lieutenant of the 6th Cavalry was John J. Pershing, newly graduated from West Point, who years later was to go on an-

Geronimo, trying to look civilized in a photographer's studio. Probably taken after his last surrender.

other chase into Mexico after Pancho Villa. They pursued the unbelievably elusive Apaches for two months, up and down mountains, in and out of canyons, until finally even the iron fugitives were worn down.

The end of it all came when Lieutenant Charles B. Gatewood, 6th Cavalry, who had often led the Apache scouts and knew their ways well, ventured ahead, with only three men, into the mountain fastnesses where Geronimo was hiding and managed to have a talk with him. It was a most courageous act, for Gatewood's life was at the mercy of the savages, but he succeeded in persuading the Indians to surrender in July, 1886. That about closed the book, with one major exception, on the ages-old story of the Indian's resistance to the ever-oncoming white man.

CHAPTER IX

Wars Beyond the Border
1890 – 1917

Historians generally agree that the year 1890, if a definite year has to be picked, marked the end of the American frontier. The buffalo was gone, the transcontinental railroads were completed, the roving Indians were corralled on reservations, virtually all of the good land had been occupied, and the open range was almost a memory. From the first settlement in Virginia in 1607, the effect of the frontier on American character had been enormous because the constant struggle against nature and savage Indians had developed the national traits of democracy, self-reliance, ingenuity and, to a certain extent, lawlessness. The frontier may have literally ended about 1890 but its spirit lives on as the golden age of romance and adventure, in the hearts and minds of Americans, and it is symbolized for eternity by the Indian, the frontiersman, the cowboy, and the cavalry trooper.

The Indians were all on reservations by 1890 but there was still restlessness and resentment in some of the incorrigibles; and as one chief scornfully said, "God made me an Indian but not a reservation Indian." In the winter of 1889–1890, a new and strange unrest bubbled to the surface among the tribes on their scattered reservations. Somewhere in Nevada, an Indian prophet had arisen, a sort of mysterious and obscure Messiah, who preached that the good old days of freedom and plentiful

Sitting Bull, taken in 1885

game were coming back. These teachings were pretty harmless in themselves but when they trickled through to Sitting Bull and the still rebellious Sioux, festering in the monotony of reservation life, they made trouble. Sitting Bull, perhaps because of the appeal of his fanciful name (although it certainly is not more bizarre than Crazy Horse), was generally associated with the Custer massacre, in which he had actually not been as important a leader as Chiefs Gall and Crazy Horse. After the massacre he and his braves had escaped to Canada but had returned to the reservation in South Dakota in 1881, after a promise of amnesty for his past misdeeds. He retained a burning hatred for the whites, and when news of the Indian Messiah in the west reached him he called a general assembly of the Sioux on a reservation in South Dakota to discuss the possibilities of another uprising.

This movement became threatening and two troops of the 8th Cavalry moved in to arrest Sitting Bull before things got out of hand. His followers attempted to rescue him and the chief was killed in the melee. The 7th Cavalry then arrived to break up the encampment and in the ensuing fight at Wounded Knee, just south of the Bad Lands, some three hundred Indians were killed. The Sioux were finally calmed down the next month and surrendered their arms; and this, once and for all, ended the troubles with that fierce and magnificent tribe of mounted warriors.

There were two more spasms of rebellion before the Indians finally accepted United States law. In 1898, the Chippewas in Minnesota had a small skirmish with troops and in 1907, the tribe of Utes in Colorado and Utah refused to send their children to school. The entire 6th Cavalry regiment was then sent in as sort of glorified truant officers to enforce the law. The picture of a tough trooper leading a kicking and squalling Ute child to school seems to ring down the curtain on the seventy-year melodrama of mounted Indian versus cavalryman. One can suspect that the sympathy of the trooper was strongly with the yelling child whom he forcibly led to an education and all its complications.

While the great drama of conquering the West was being played, there were cavalrymen exploring other frontiers. In 1883, Lieutenant Fred Schwatka, of the 3rd Cavalry, led a party of seven men to the headwaters of the Yukon River in Canada and descended its whole length through Alaska by raft and boat. Two years later, Lieutenant Henry T. Allen, 2nd Cavalry, later a major general in World War I, explored the upper reaches of the Copper River in Alaska and pushed on north to the Arctic Circle.

The big name in Arctic exploration, however, was Lieutenant Adolphus Washington Greely, of the 5th Cavalry. He was a native of Newburyport, Massachusetts, who had risen from private to major during the Civil War, and had received a post-war appointment as first lieutenant. While serving on the frontier, Greely had constructed about 2000 miles of telegraph lines, during the late 1870's, in Texas, Dakota, and Montana. In 1881 he headed an expedition to the Arctic which established an observation post, called Fort Conger, on the northeast coast of Ellsmere Island, just across the narrow strait from the extreme northwestern tip of Greenland. Two army officers, Lieutenants Lockwood and Brainard, on an exploring trip from this base, reached latitude 83° 24', the farthest north up to that time. The party returned southward in August, 1883, and reached Cape Sabine with great difficulty.

UGLY

A KICKER

A REARER

A STEADY GOER

A PLUNGER

ANOTHER KICKER

Harper's Weekly, *Feb. 15, 1890.*
Harvard College Library

"Training Army Horses to Stand Fire,"
by Frederic Remington

In the meanwhile efforts had been made by relief ships to reach the expedition but these had failed to get through. Greely and his men, whose supplies were about exhausted, were forced to spend another winter in the north, and during this time all but seven of the original twenty-five died of cold and starvation. Hope had about been given up when a relief ship arrived in June, 1884, and rescued the survivors under the most dramatic circumstances. The ship had searched all probable places and sent parties over the ice without success. One of Greely's dying men thought he heard a steamer's whistle, and the only two

"Stable Call," by Rufus F. Zogbaum

Horse, Foot, and Dragoons.
Boston Public Library

men who could walk stumbled out of the shelter to see. The whistle had been sounded to recall the last search party and Greely's two men were fortunately seen. If the ship had arrived a day or so later not a man would have been found alive. Greely later was awarded the Congressional Medal of Honor and became Chief Signal Officer and a major general. It was a far cry from the Texas plains to the Arctic Circle but a cavalryman rose to the opportunity.

Life became a routine affair in the cavalry regiments after the taming of the Indians. For the first time in nearly fifty years, peace and quiet reigned on the plains and in the mountains; and the mounted service had a chance to catch its breath and relax in the more leisurely tempo of garrison life. However, no sooner had peace descended on the wide open spaces than labor disputes and disorders broke out in the cities and industrial centers, and, between the years 1886 and 1895, the army was used to preserve order in 328 civil troubles in forty-nine states and territories. The cavalry bore its fair share of these disagreeable tasks, in which, however, there was fortunately little or no bloodshed. The next real fighting came when the war clouds which had been gathering over Cuba for years broke into the full storm of the Spanish-American War in 1898.

Just as the average American mentally groups all the Indian wars around the shadowy figure of George Armstrong Custer and his last stand, so does he seem to tie in the Spanish-American War with Theodore Roosevelt and his Rough Riders charging up San Juan Hill. The Rough Riders received more publicity than they probably deserved; but their colorful backgrounds and personalities, plus their young, prominent, aggressive, dashing, and very popular leader, Teddy Roosevelt, who was always in an aura of publicity, won the personal interest and attention

217

of the leading war correspondents, such as Richard Harding Davis and John Fox, Jr., with the result that Roosevelt and his Rough Riders completely stole the show of the Spanish-American War. The name itself stirred memories of the gallant Allan McLane and his original band of Rough Riders harassing the British in Philadelphia during the Revolutionary War.

The Rough Riders — or "Teddy's Terrors," as they were sometimes called — had the official name of the 1st United States Volunteer Cavalry and were mostly recruited in the four remaining territories of the time, Arizona, New Mexico, Oklahoma, and Indian Territory, with about a half coming from New Mexico alone. Colonel Leonard Wood, who had served so well against the Apaches, was the commanding officer until just before San Juan Hill, when he was promoted to brigadier general. He was succeeded by Roosevelt, who had been lieutenant colonel, but the regiment has always been linked with the latter in the public mind. The men were largely cowboys or prospectors who were used to horses and life in the open. Mixed with these frontiersmen was a small leavening of socially and athletically prominent Eastern college men from the Big Three of Yale, Harvard, and Princeton. The feelings of the western newspapers were mixed about this effete infusion. The *Denver Evening Post* announced in headlines, "DUDES ARE ALL RIGHT, CURLED DARLINGS OF SOCIETY JOIN TEDDY'S TERRORS," and the Santa Fe *New Mexican* noted approvingly that "The New York swells, who enlisted in the 1st Regiment of U. S. Volunteer Cavalry, had to leave their valets at home"; but a while later this newspaper expressed concern for the western way of life by saying: "There is some local fear . . . that the simple manners and customs of the New Mexico cowboy may be contam-

Photograph taken in Cuba during the Spanish-American War. In the foreground, from left to right: General Joseph Wheeler, Colonel Leonard Wood, and Lieutenant Colonel Theodore Roosevelt.

inated and his morals deteriorated by contact with these New Yorkers."

The Rough Riders, cowboys and dudes, were assembled at San Antonio, Texas, in May, 1898. Incidentally, they were dressed in the new regulation uniform. The old all-blue outfit had given way to khaki breeches and blouses but a blue shirt was retained and this was often set off, in the field, by a red bandanna around the neck. The uncorrupted New Mexican cowboys had been waylaid en route by some pretty girls serving coffee at a stop at Gainesville, Texas, who were so winsome that they snagged all the brass buttons in sight, and the New Mexicans arrived at the rendezvous with their blouses held together by horseshoe nails. There seemed to be some question about who was corrupting whom during the short training period of about a month, in San Antonio. The regiment was quartered at the fair ground in Riverside Park (now Roosevelt Park), a few miles south of the city. Officially, all were supposed to remain in quarters during the night but the New Mexican contingent soon found a loose board in the surrounding fence, and, with the unofficial connivance of their elected officers, spent many a pleasant evening in the city's beer halls. There was considerable excitement one night at a nearby band concert when the selection "Custer's Last Stand" was rendered, during which the band members, following the score, fired several shots. One trooper, his memories evidently stirred by this fusillade, joined in the spirit of the occasion, and blazed away at an electric light. Immediately every light in the place was shot out by his exuberant comrades. The band scrammed, women screamed, and one of the local newspapers printed a scathing editorial about the wild Rough Riders.

The somewhat informal state of discipline in this regiment was illustrated by Trooper Lewis, who,

> lounging with the rest of the guard, heard the corporal call, Attention! casually laid his newspaper aside, and, still sprawling, observed with satisfaction the trim figure of Colonel Wood. When the colonel had passed, the corporal spoke his mind.
>
> "Why didn't yo' jump up an' salute, yo' jay?" he bawled. "Didn't yo' hear me shout Attention?"
>
> "Sure, I did," said the trooper. "I thought yo' jest wanted me to look alive to somethin' interestin'." *

The troopers met their horses in San Antonio, which were mostly unbroken but were welcomed like long-lost friends. The first attempt at drill with these mustangs was a veritable shambles, a free-for-all, with bucking broncos and unhorsed troopers scattered all over the drill ground. But the experienced cowboys soon broke their mounts into reasonable obedience although there was always a half-hour tussle in the morning before they could get down to the serious business of the day. One morning, after hours of work getting the green horses into a quiet line, a trooper, to celebrate the event, fired his six-shooter into the ground. There was an immediate stampede, with some horses and riders ending up in the creek at the end of the parade ground. Toward the end of May, a review of the regiment was held in honor of a high-ranking regular army officer. Much effort was expended on spit and polish for this gala affair but the officer concluded the festivities by saying he had never seen anything worse in his life.

The Rough Riders entrained for Tampa, Florida, in late May, and, after running headlong into a state of unbelievable con-

* Hermann Hagedorn, *Leonard Wood, A Biography* (New York, 1931).

221

fusion and mismanagement at that port, they embarked for Cuba by simply seizing and boarding, and then holding against all comers, an unguarded transport which had previously been assigned to two other regiments. The horses, except those of the officers, were left behind in care of the disgusted and disappointed men of one squadron.

The transports, after the wild free-for-all of each regiment for itself in embarking, then sweltered at anchor for several days in the burning heat of Tampa harbor; the old story of hurry, hurry — wait! Finally the convoy got under way and nine days later a go-as-you-please landing was made on the south coast of Cuba, near Santiago, in whose harbor the Spanish fleet under Cervera was blockaded by an American squadron. What horses there were on the transports were cast overboard and forced to swim ashore, in which process one of the two belonging to Colonel Roosevelt was drowned. The landing of the men was made haphazardly in ships' boats but the Rough Riders all made it safely, although a boat carrying colored soldiers from another transport capsized and two men drowned.

The Rough Riders, after landing, became a part of the cavalry division under the command of the gallant old Confederate cavalryman Major General Joseph Wheeler, who was later reported to have unconsciously referred, in the heat of battle, to the Spanish enemy as "damn Yankees." The other regiments in the division were all regulars: the 1st, 3rd, 6th, and the colored 9th and 10th Cavalry. This division pushed ahead on foot into the dense jungle and soon made contact with the Spaniards, with a resulting sharp encounter in which the division, with 964 men engaged, lost sixteen killed and fifty-two wounded, and of this number eight were killed and thirty-four wounded among the Rough Riders.

*How the Rough Riders did NOT charge up San Juan Hill.
The only man mounted was Colonel Roosevelt, who dismounted when stopped by a wire fence and led his men
to the summit on foot. The artist, W. G. Read, however,
produced a hell-for-leather cavalry charge.*

About a week later, the cavalry division stormed and captured
San Juan Hill, a strongly fortified position defending Santiago.
Colonel Roosevelt, on horseback, led his men up the hill until
he was stopped by a wire fence near the summit, when he dismounted and went on afoot. It was an exuberant and spontaneous sort of charge, without much order, with men of the 1st
and the colored 9th Cavalry mixing in with the Rough Riders
for the final spurt. Nowadays there seems to be a tendency to

Colonel Theodore Roosevelt and a group of
Rough Riders on San Juan Hill after the battle

look on that charge as a sort of comic-opera affair. In reality it
was a tough fight with heavy losses. If anything, the Rough
Riders were too eager and dashed ahead rashly and precipi-
tately. The regiment numbered 490 men, and of these eighty-
nine were killed or wounded — a casualty list which is anything
but comic. The cavalry division, all told, numbered some 2300

officers and men, of whom 375 were killed and wounded. Dismounted, they carried earthworks which were defended by veteran Spanish infantry with the best modern Mauser rifles, and won a very creditable victory.

Santiago surrendered shortly afterwards and all fighting ended in September. The cavalry division suffered nearly as much from the climate and tropical fevers, chiefly malaria, as it did from the Spaniards; and the hospital and medical facilities were woefully inadequate. Also there was the threat of a real yellow fever epidemic. The rations were atrociously bad and there were resultant scandals about the inedible embalmed and canned beef supplied to the troops. The War Department finally ordered the seriously fever-ridden cavalry division back to Montauk Point, Long Island, to recuperate; and it landed there in mid-August. The usual confusion reigned in the home-coming, as well; in fact, the whole Spanish-American War was so dreadfully mismanaged that it aroused the country to reforms and innovations in the mossbacked bureaucracy of the War Department which paid dividends later on.

The Rough Riders found that the hospital furnished the best beds and food at Montauk Point, and the regiment for a while went on the sick list nearly en masse. Then the lure of New York overcame the desire for creature comforts and the regiment experienced a remarkable recovery to go on pass to the big city where the men were wined and dined with munificent hospitality. Those who remained around the camp added to their incomes by winning wagers in riding the outlaw broncos of the neighboring regular cavalry regiments. A month after the return the regiment was mustered out and at that occasion presented their popular commanding officer with a statuette especially modeled by Frederic Remington, "The Bronco-Buster."

By itself, Theodore Roosevelt's record as commanding officer of the Rough Riders may not have landed him in the White House — but it certainly helped. He was always immensely popular in the West and he kept in touch with all the old Rough Riders, some of whom occasionally strayed into difficulties with the law. Years later, while President, he ran across one of his old troopers who had just served a term in jail for shooting his mother-in-law. President Roosevelt, concerned with the moral aspect, asked him how he did it. The culprit, thinking his old commanding officer was interested in the technical angle, replied cheerfully. "Oh, I used a thirty-eight on a forty-five frame."

Roosevelt Collection. Harvard College Library

Rough Riders shooting craps at Montauk Point.
Small boy unknown.

While the fighting was going on in Cuba, the army landed an expeditionary force of about 10,000 men in the Philippines to take over from Admiral Dewey's fleet, which had defeated the Spanish squadron and captured the Spanish naval base at Cavite. Major General Wesley Merritt commanded this force which captured the city of Manila in mid-August. Merritt had been one of Sheridan's most able young cavalry leaders during the Civil War. Graduating from West Point in 1860, he had served with the old 2nd Dragoons and as aide-de-camp to General Philip St. George Cooke, commanding the cavalry of the Army of the Potomac, during the first part of the war. After that, Merritt's rise had been rapid, equaling that of his contemporaries Custer and Mackenzie; and he, like them, had ended the war as a major general of volunteers while still in his middle twenties. After the war he had become lieutenant colonel of the new colored 9th Cavalry; and about ten years later the colonel of the 5th Cavalry. He had served with distinction during the Indian wars and was the only one of Sheridan's lieutenants to live on to serve in the Spanish-American War. After the capture of Manila, he became the first American military governor of the Philippines but was soon sent to Paris to attend the peace conference which officially ended the war in December, 1898.

New troubles broke out in the Philippines in early 1899 when the Filipino insurgents who had been fighting the Spaniards turned upon the occupying American troops when it became clear that the latter were there to stay. Major General (Fighting Joe) Wheeler, on his return from Cuba, was sent to the Philippines to command a brigade of infantry, but after his arrival there he asked for cavalry which would be more useful in the guerrilla warfare which broke out throughout the islands. After some delay, most of the 4th Cavalry arrived in the autumn of 1899 and by June, 1901, there were eight regular cavalry regiments on hand. The 11th U. S. Volunteer Cavalry was organized in Manila in the late summer of 1899, and Captain James Lockett of the 4th Cavalry was made its colonel. He asked for and obtained as squadron commanders two West Point football stars, Thomas G. Carson and Dennis A. Nolan (later a major general in World War I), who did wonders with this regiment. Also a squadron of volunteer cavalry was raised among the Filipinos which was naturally of great value. This was primarily a second lieutenant's war because of the constant fighting and skirmishing by the scattered small garrisons and detachments in the jungle and back country. In this nasty fighting the old cavalryman Major General Henry W. Lawton, a Civil War veteran, who had been one of Ranald Mackenzie's officers in the 4th Cavalry on the plains of Texas, was killed. The war practically ended with the capture of the insurgent leader Aguinaldo in March, 1901.

No sooner had the Christian Filipino insurgents been conquered than the Moslem Moros of the southern islands rebelled. This people was hostile to all Christians and had fought for years against the Spaniards and Filipinos and it was said that they delayed rebellion against the Americans because they did not recognize them as Christians — or, at least, the kind of Christians they knew. There was some hard fighting in this local war because the Moros were the most fanatical and dangerous warriors of the islands. Two young cavalry officers, Captains John J. Pershing and Frank R. McCoy, both later to become generals, led successful expeditions into the heart of the Moro country which finally helped to bring peace.

Another little war in the Orient in which the cavalry played

*General Henry W. Lawton, an "Old Army" cavalryman
who was killed in the Philippines*

a part was the Boxer Uprising in China in 1900. This was an anti-foreign affair in which the rebellious Boxers besieged the foreign legations in the capital, Peking. An expeditionary force made up of troops from the eight great powers finally cut their way through to the relief of the legations. Two squadrons of the 6th Cavalry formed part of the American contingent which was commanded by Major General Adna Ramanza Chaffee, an old cavalryman since Civil War days. This was the first war since the Revolution in which the army co-operated with allies.

The enlarged responsibilities which the peace with Spain brought us, to maintain order in the former Spanish possessions, caused Congress to authorize an increase in the regular army in February, 1901. By this act, four new regiments of cavalry were created, the 11th through the 15th, and the troops of all the cavalry regiments were given a flexible strength from 100 to 164 men, as the President, as Commander-in-Chief, might direct.

Again there was a short interim of peace and quiet after the troubles in the Far East simmered down. The cavalry pursued a routine garrison existence for almost a decade in the Philippines, the Hawaiian Islands, and the West, which was made more pleasurable by the game of polo which not only was enjoyed for itself but also served to improve horsemanship and the breed of mounts. During this time the blue shirt of the Spanish-American War was discarded and replaced by the present all-khaki or olive-drab uniform. There were a few incidents which broke this regular life, two in the year 1906: the San Francisco earthquake and fire in April, at which the old cavalryman and famous Arctic explorer General Adolphus Washington Greely had command of the armed forces, including two cavalry regiments, which were rushed in to preserve order and bring relief to the sufferers; the other being an intervention in Cuba — which lasted for three years — in which two cavalry regiments formed a part of the occupying force.

In 1916 there were serious labor troubles in the Colorado mine fields and the 11th and 12th Cavalry regiments were sent in at the request of the governor to restore order and remained there for nine months. The colorful and famous Mother Jones was there as a labor leader, and a great deal of damage to the mine properties had been done before the arrival of these regiments; but they had no difficulty during their stay. The most

230

enduring memory of some of the cavalrymen was not the strike, or Mother Jones, but one particular guard mount. A sergeant of the 11th had as a rather unusual pet a huge diamond-back rattlesnake whose fangs he had extracted. His fellow troopers did not take kindly to his zoological whim and planned to get rid of the snake when the sergeant mounted guard. Hearing of this, the sergeant placed the snake inside his campaign shirt. When the officer of the guard, Lieutenant George H. Timmins, now living in Groton, Massachusetts, inspected his detail, he took the sergeant's gun from port arms, at which point the rattler thrust out his head toward Timmins to inspect him in turn; with the result that the lieutenant dropped the gun amidst a scene of considerable confusion in the ranks.

In 1910, President Porfirio Diaz of Mexico — the grand old man or the implacable tyrant, depending on one's point of view — who had been dictator for nearly thirty-five years, abdicated his office and left the country. Whatever else he had done, he had certainly brought law and order, peace and quiet to that previously turbulent land. All hell immediately erupted upon his departure and Mexico was torn with revolutions and drenched with blood for the next ten years, probably an averaging up for the long period of peace during Diaz's rule. The internecine fighting among the Mexican factions became so threatening to American lives and property that troops were rushed to the border in 1911, and the cavalry, in particular, was concentrated there for years afterwards. The deep-seated hatred against the *gringo* in the hearts of most Mexicans of all factions, was intensified by various events, and particularly by the United States occupation of the port of Vera Cruz in April, 1914. The most virulent anti-American leader was Pancho Villa. One of his officers gave a practical demonstration of this feeling by tak-

Pancho Villa

ing eighteen Americans off a train in the winter of 1916 and shooting them. Secretary of State William J. Bryan, that Puritan moralist, however, rather favored Villa, at least from the moral side, because Villa neither smoked nor drank, but Villa, probably, had been so busy murdering, raping, and looting that he had never had time to take up the minor vices.

Wars Beyond the Border

In the winter of 1916, the 13th Cavalry was stationed at the little border hamlet of Columbus, New Mexico, through which ran the main line of the Southern Pacific Railroad from El Paso, Texas, to the West. "Life at Columbus was not exciting," wrote Lieutenant John P. Lucas. "There was little to do and plenty of time to do it in." * Lucas described the heat and monotony of the sun-baked little desert town, the habit of rattlesnakes to occupy the houses, and the fact that the nearest tree was in El Paso, seventy-five miles away. He went on to say:

> Three exciting events took place during my sojourn at Columbus. First, the "Golden States" [the crack passenger train of the Southern Pacific] passed through every day going east. This occurrence was attended regularly by all those present for duty. Second, the "Golden States" passed through every day going west. This was attended also by all those present for duty. Third, Villa raided the camp and town on March 9, 1916. This, likewise, was attended by all those present for duty.

Villa slipped over the border with some 500 to 1000 followers and hit the sleeping town at about four o'clock in the morning. The sentries of the 13th Cavalry were on the alert, however, in the camp area just south of the town, and a general engagement broke out along the main street. The Mexicans foolishly set fire to the hotel, which lit up themselves as easy targets to the dismounted troopers who had been quickly assembled by their officers, and a deadly fire was poured into the *Villistas* which soon drove them out of the town. The Mexican casualties were high, for sixty-seven dead raiders were found and burned the next day; the brush and mesquite were full of them. The American losses were seven soldiers killed, five wounded; and eight civilians killed and two wounded.

* Frank Tompkins, *Chasing Villa* (Harrisburg, 1934).

PLAN TO SEND A FORCE INTO MEXICO TO PUNISH VILLA RAIDERS FOR KILLING 17 AMERICANS IN COLUMBUS, NEW MEXICO

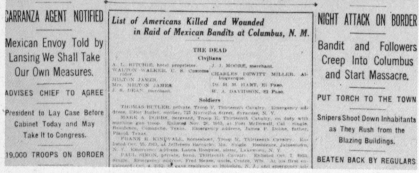

CARRANZA AGENT NOTIFIED

Mexican Envoy Told by Lansing We Shall Take Our Own Measures.

ADVISES CHIEF TO AGREE

President to Lay Case Before Cabinet Today and May Take It to Congress.

19,000 TROOPS ON BORDER

List of Americans Killed and Wounded in Raid of Mexican Bandits at Columbus, N. M.

THE DEAD
Civilians

NIGHT ATTACK ON BORDER

Bandit and Followers Creep Into Columbus and Start Massacre.

PUT TORCH TO THE TOWN

Snipers Shoot Down Inhabitants as They Rush from the Blazing Buildings.

BEATEN BACK BY REGULARS

Headline, New York Times, *March 10, 1916*

Major Frank Tompkins gathered together a mounted detachment of thirty-two men and pursued the retreating *Villistas* across the border and by intelligent harassing tactics managed to kill from seventy-five to one hundred more as they galloped away to the south. It had been a costly foray for Villa and it made him a fugitive for months to come.

Some of the Americans, however, had harrowing experiences. A few of the officers and their families lived in the western end of the town which was first overrun by the raiders. Captain R. E. Smyser, with his wife and two children, climbed out a window and hid in an outhouse when the Mexicans hammered at their front door. They soon abandoned this for the mesquite, where they were well filled with cactus thorns. Smyser eagerly joined in the pursuit later, spurred on by these wounds. One young lieutenant, his wife, young daughter, another officer, and

234

a soldier also hid in the mesquite where they were discovered by a retreating Mexican. They wounded him with a shotgun and pulled him into their hiding place; but their narrow escapes from discovery by the retreating Mexicans were harrowing to an extreme. A Mrs. Moore, wounded in the leg, whose husband had been killed and house set afire, was found crawling in the mesquite by Major Tompkins and his pursuing detachment. She was taken to the hospital and afterwards recovered. When the first wave of Mexicans hit the camp area, several of the kitchen crews were surrounded in their mess shacks. These fought off the raiders with the shotguns kept on hand to shoot quail or rabbits, and in one shack the crew used a large pot of boiling water, axes, and a baseball bat not only to repel but to kill a few of the raiders.

This outrageous attack was too much for even the Woodrow Wilson administration, which had been handling the explosive Mexican situation with a mixture of patience and petulance; and a punitive expedition was immediately organized under the command of Brigadier General John J. Pershing, who had seen so much service in the Indian wars and in the Philippines. The administration, however, did all it could to hamper the pursuit of Villa, for strict orders were issued that the Mexican railroads and telegraph lines could not be used or towns passed through without the permission of the *de facto* Carranza government, a faction which then held the capital and against which Villa had been fighting. The *Carranzistas* were but a shade less anti-American than their opponents and almost always refused the use of the railroads or to co-operate in any way. In fact, a while later, there was about as much fighting against these hoped-for allies as there was against the followers of the villain of the piece, the elusive Pancho Villa.

General Pershing's force crossed the border on March 15th. It was primarily a cavalry expedition with supporting infantry, artillery, and various service detachments; it included, at one time or another, all or parts of the 5th, 6th, 7th, 10th, 11th, 12th, and 13th cavalry regiments. There was also an aero squadron of the Signal Corps attached, and the planes were largely used to carry messages. This was their first appearance in a campaign by our army, but they were not much of a success, because the serviceable planes soon cracked up in the rough Mexican country where replacements and repairs were not possible. The motor trucks used were not satisfactory bcause of the rough terrain, and the old-fashioned horse- or mule-drawn wagons became the chief reliance on the supply lines — a condition which conceivably might exist again in similar country. One of the acting aides-de-camp to General Pershing was First Lieutenant George S. Patton, Jr., of the 8th Cavalry, who was on special service with the expedition.

The punitive expedition set up headquarters about 120 miles south of the border in the Mexican state of Chihuahua and several flying cavalry columns were sent out to the south to trail Villa and bring him in dead or alive. These columns were cut off from any base and had to live off the country in the way of the old cavalry in the Indian wars. This was, in fact, the last campaign of the old cavalry, and its achievements, considering the handicaps imposed from Washington, were remarkably good. The columns rode, each horse carrying about 250 pounds, through the daytime heat, hot wind, and dust of the Chihuahua desert and at night shivered in the freezing cold of the high altitude. Their routes south paralleled, to the west and in much rougher country, that taken by Colonel Doniphan and his Mounted Missouri Volunteers on their march in the winter of

1847 to capture Chihuahua City. They never captured Villa, largely because of the stupid restrictions placed upon them, but they fought several engagements with bands of his followers, defeated and dispersed them, and killed several of his most able lieutenants; and Villa's fangs were drawn for the time being. If the *Carranzistas* had co-operated, or if the cavalry had been allowed a free hand, it would probably have caught Villa; for he was said to have been badly wounded in a recent fight with the *Carranzistas* and to have been recuperating in a mountain hideout.

National Archives

The chase after Villa. Brigadier General John J. Pershing crossing the Santa Maria River in Mexico.

One of the columns, a small one of two troops of the 13th Cavalry, commanded by Major Frank Tompkins, who had ridden out after Villa from the shambles in Columbus, reached as far south as Parral, a city of about 20,000, which lies almost 150 miles south of the city of Chihuahua. Tompkins and his men approached Parral in the belief that they would be welcomed by the authorities there, and with pleasurable visions of hot baths and long, cool drinks in this oasis of civilization; but they were treacherously attacked there by a large force of *Carranzistas*, their nominal friends, and forced to retreat northward. From then on, the whole countryside, *Villistas* and *Carranzistas*, were against the invading *gringos* and, to conform to Woodrow Wilson's Mexican policy of peace at almost any price, the punitive expedition gradually withdrew northward until it recrossed the border in February, 1917 — without Villa.

There were several other engagements with the Mexicans. At the town of Guerrero, Colonel George A. Dodd and the 7th Cavalry, after a night's march in freezing weather, over a precipitous mountain trail, made an early morning attack on a large band of *Villistas*, killed the commanding officer, and drove them head-

National Archives
The Seventh Cavalry passing in review at Dublan, Mexico

long from the place with heavy losses. On the debit side was the famous affair at Carrizal in June where a large force of *Carranzistas* met two troops of the colored 10th Cavalry, killed two officers and ten men, wounded eleven others, and captured twenty-three troopers who were afterwards safely returned. There is a monument today on the site of this fight which describes this "glorious Mexican victory" in rather redundant words.

There was one individual exploit which reflected creditably on the pistol marksmanship of Lieutenant George S. Patton, years later to be called by his men in North Africa and Sicily "Pistol Packing Patton" because of the pair of conspicuous pearl-handled revolvers he always wore. One wonders if they really knew what an expert he was in their use. Patton went out one day to buy forage with seven men in three automobiles. They approached a large ranch house which belonged to a colonel of the Villa forces. Something led Patton to suspect that the colonel might be home on a visit; and he distributed his men to cover all exits of the large house, which was built around a patio, with Patton alone watching the front gate. His hunch proved

National Archives

An escort wagon pulling a stalled truck across the Santa Maria River near El Valle, Mexico. The motor vehicles were of little use.

Indian Scouts at El Valle, Mexico, First Lieutenant James A. Shannon, Eleventh Cavalry, commanding. Photographed some time between July 7 and October 1, 1916. Shannon later was mortally wounded at Chatel Chehery in the Argonne on October 8, 1918. He was a quarterback on the West Point football team and then on duty at Harvard College before going to Mexico.

correct, for three horsemen, armed with rifles and pistols, emerged at a gallop from the front entrance. As orders prohibited firing until hostile identification was certain, Patton held his fire until the men turned and fired at him. He then returned the fire with his pistol and killed all three men, one of whom proved to be the long-sought-for *Villista* colonel.

While all this campaigning went on in Mexico, the National Guard, to the strength of 150,000 men was called out for service on the border. When the punitive expedition returned from Mexico in February, 1917, it found the border for once adequately protected against any further threat of raids or forays. The war with Germany began that following April, and the National Guard was largely withdrawn for service elsewhere and overseas. But the Cavalry, with the exception of one regiment, remained on the Mexican border to watch the ever-present danger from the south.

CHAPTER X

The Twilight

1917 – 1942

WHILE PERSHING'S CAVALRYMEN were chasing the will-o'-the-wisp Pancho Villa through the deserts and mountains of northern Mexico, Congress passed the National Defense Act in June, 1916, which at last established a definite military policy and supplanted a host of fragmentary and confusing acts of previous years. This long-overdue act authorized an increase in strength for the cavalry of from fifteen to twenty-five regiments, each to be composed of twelve troops plus a machine-gun troop. Before this could be effected, our entry into World War I, in April, 1917, interrupted the program, and the cavalry entered the war with only seventeen regiments.

The western front in France had been stabilized and deadlocked for over two and a half years in a trench warfare in which there were huge casualties and little change of position, and there was no use there for the arm of movement, the cavalry. Incidentally this was not true of the fighting on the eastern front, where the war was much more fluid and where both the Russians and the Austro-Germans used large numbers of mounted troops; nor was it true of the fighting in the Near East where General Allenby's successes against the Turks were largely gained by his British and Indian cavalry.

Then, there was the ever-present threat from a bitterly resentful Mexico to the south, a country which, despite its con-

Military Polo Champions of the World. Four officers of the United States Army who defeated the British Army polo players in two games out of three. Left to right: Major A. H. Wilson, Cav.; Maj. J. K. Herr, Cav.; Lt. Col. Lewis Brown, Cav.; Maj. L. Beard, Q.M.C.

tinuing bloody internecine revolutions and counterrevolutions, was always ready to unite against the hated *gringos* and to encourage raids across the border in retaliation for what it considered the violation of its sovereignty by the expedition after Villa. Mexico was full of German agents, as well, who did all in their power to stir up feeling against the United States among a responsive people and bring about a war which would have been an embarrassing distraction to say the least. And so the bulk of our cavalry force was left on the border to cope with an extremely dangerous situation which, if it had broken into flames, might well have jeopardized all our efforts against Germany in Europe.

One regiment only, the 2nd Cavalry, went overseas. This was given the thankless and uncongenial task of running various remount stations where a great number of mules and horses, used for transport, were cared for. However, in August, 1918, when it became evident that the Germans had about shot their bolt and that a war of movement might be in the offing, a provisional squadron was hastily organized for combat duty. General E. N. Harmon, later to win distinction in World War II as a leader of our armored forces, but then a captain in the 2nd Cavalry, says that the widely scattered troopers were assembled within fifteen days and mounted on a veritable hodge-podge of animals, gleaned from the remount stations and veterinary hospitals, which varied in type from a Percheron draft horse to a Spanish pony; and, of this motley herd, forty-two were white or gray, which were highly conspicuous for enemy fire. One feels that the spirits of Don Quixote, mounted on Rosinante, and Sancho Panza, on his burro, rode with these tilters after windmills. This impromptu squadron rode out to take part in the September offensive of the Allies, and the troopers were used for liaison, reconnaissance, and for pursuit of the retreating Germans. The squadron captured a number of prisoners, including a German staff officer riding a large and handsome black horse which Captain Harmon then rode for the rest of the campaign. A German general, mounted on an even better horse, unfortunately just barely escaped capture.

Despite the small part played by the cavalry in the trench warfare of the western front, all the great generals of the conflict, including Allenby, Haig, Ludendorff, and Pétain, were emphatic in stating their belief in its value for a campaign of movement. General Pershing summed it up by saying: "There is not in the world today, an officer of distinction, recognized as an authority on military matters in a broad way, who does not declare with emphasis that cavalry is as important today as it ever has been."

And this was not just the whistling in the dark of an old cavalryman. Pershing had just been in the field after Villa and had had fresh and firsthand experience in a campaign of movement and action. He alone of all the Allied generals had seen both types of warfare within a year and was certainly fitted to draw an intelligent conclusion.

After the war, the usual economy drive hit the army and the cavalry bore its full share of cuts and mutilations. The number of regiments was reduced from seventeen to fourteen by inactivating the three bearing the highest numbers. In 1921 the remaining fourteen regiments were reduced to half strength by placing certain squadrons and troops on an inactive status. The First Cavalry Division was nominally retained as a unit but it was whittled down to only the absolutely necessary personnel and units in headquarters, and to two brigades of two skeletonized cavalry regiments each, a battalion of horse artillery, a mounted engineer battalion, and an ambulance company.

The officers of the regular cavalry, many now without a regimental assignment, were employed to train the National Guard and the Cavalry Reserve units. The outstanding enthusiasts in horsemanship turned eagerly to the field of mounted sports to continue the progress in equitation interrupted by the war. The National Guard units, such as Squadron A in New York, the Light Horse Troop in Philadelphia, the Essex Troop in New Jersey, and others throughout the country, responded to this

First Army manuevers in the Carolinas ... Coming down over the cliff, Troop B, 102nd Cavalry, the Essex Troop of Newark, N.J. November 14, 1941.

*Fort Riley, Kansas. Second Cavalry troopers astride horses
swimming the Smoky Hill River, October 11, 1940.*

program with great enthusiasm; and there was an upsurge of interest in fox hunting, polo, steeplechasing, and in the competition of horse shows. Squadron A of New York opened its new armory in 1921 to which the annual horse show moved from Madison Square Garden, and this building became a center for all mounted sports and events. All these sports kept the officers fit and alert, and furnished a welcome antidote to the routine of garrison life; and, with the color and splendor of mounted reviews and parades, furnished a glamour to service in the cavalry lacking in the other branches. There was never a dull moment; all worked hard and played hard. Overseas, in the army of occupation in Germany, Major General Henry T. Allen (who as a young lieutenant had explored the upper reaches of the Copper River in Alaska) encouraged his officers and men to maintain a scarlet-coated hunt team, several polo teams, and strings of horses for races and horse shows which successfully competed in inter-Allied meets with the French and British at Coblenz, Wiesbaden, and Cologne. The cavalry regiments in Hawaii and the Philippines also showed the same enthusiasms and built up a tremendous popular interest in horses and mounted sports.

These activities soon began to show results as army horsemen swept the boards in all our prominent horse shows and furnished the equitation teams for the Olympic Games. The Chief of Staff, General Peyton L. March, and his successor General Pershing, were both enthusiasts for these mounted sports and wholeheartedly supported them. Polo was officially approved as a sport which developed the qualities so valuable to combat officers in war, and wisely so, for it graduated such men as Patton, Truscott, Wainwright, Terry Allen, Paddy Flint, and many others who later became outstanding leaders in battle.

Years later, in July, 1945, General Patton wrote: "I certainly hope we can restore polo for the whole army. I agree with you that polo and football are the two best sporting preparations for battle."

In 1923, the Army Polo Team won the Junior Championship at Narragansett Pier and then went on to defeat a heavily favored British Army Polo Team, composed of international players including the great Vivian Lockett, for the international military championship at Meadowbrook, Long Island. This was a great upset, for the British had been touted for an easy victory; and Meadowbrook was astounded when the Americans defeated a 34-goal British team in the final game by a score of 10 to 3 on the flat.

In January, 1933, the cavalry, in accord with General Douglas MacArthur's policy as Chief of Staff that each arm should mechanize to the greatest extent needed to execute its mission, dismounted and experimentally mechanized the 1st Cavalry regiment at Fort Knox, Kentucky; and afterwards the 13th Cavalry was added to form a mechanized brigade. A while later, on the recommendation of the Chief of Cavalry, the 4th and 6th Regiments were transformed into Horse-Mechanized Corps Reconnaissance Regiments (the usual long name) which combined the advantages of both means of transportation. A squad of eight men and eight horses, with forage and rations and complete equipment, including light and heavy machine guns in pack, could be loaded on a truck and its trailer in from five to seven minutes. The idea was for these units to use fast motor transportation where roads were available and then for the troopers to unload their horses, mount, and scout the country when the going became too rough for trucks, or, when necessary, to reconnoiter laterally off to the sides of the road itself. The success of this experiment was such that most of the remaining National Guard cavalry regiments were transformed into seven of these regiments and assigned to the appropriate corps. But the necessary equipment for this change-over was not delivered until late in 1941 and there was no chance to prove its worth in maneuvers before Pearl Harbor in December.

Horse-mechanized reconnaissance cavalry about to be loaded on truck-tractors with semitrailers

By 1940, the two mechanized regiments, the 1st and 13th, had been merged with various infantry tank battalions to form a Provisional Armored Corps and were lost to the cavalry, which was then reduced to twelve regiments, including the two which were horse-mechanized. There were also a regiment of Philippine Scouts, the 26th, which later performed magnificently in covering the retreat to Bataan, eighteen regiments in the National Guard, and officer cadres in the Organized Reserves for twenty-four unorganized regiments.

The mounted cavalry made its last appearance in strength during the Louisiana maneuvers in the autumn and winter of 1940–1941, in which two regular cavalry divisions and a brigade (56th) of the Texas National Guard took part. It was felt, by many, and with considerable bitterness, that these maneuvers were rigged to limit the activities of the cavalry, for the pressure was on from certain quarters to eliminate the mounted service. Whether intentional or not, artificial restrictions were imposed which would have been an absurdity in real warfare. The opposing armies were placed about one hundred miles apart and not allowed to move toward each other until a given time. This, of course, chained the cavalry from operating in its normal forward area where it could ambush approaching enemy infantry or mechanized columns; and, when the signal was given, both sides rushed forward in motor trucks to occupy as much ground as possible with no need to beware of hostile cavalry.

The champing cavalry naturally was unable to match the speed of the motorized columns on the roads and was compelled to operate on the flanks. Despite its shackling, it astounded its critics. On one maneuver the First Cavalry Division marched forty-four miles in twenty hours, crossed the swiftly flowing Sabine River, and delivered a decisive attack against the oppos-

The end of the trail. Troopers moving pack horses into bivouac area. Fort Bliss, Texas, April 19, 1943. First Machine Gun Squadron, Troop B, Eighth Regiment.

ing army's communications. On another occasion, after marching seventy-one miles in thirty-five hours, it crossed the same river, swollen to a depth of ten feet, and established a bridgehead for the crossing and deployment of the First Armored Corps. The rumor, at the time, was that these exploits won the horse cavalry a reprieve from the extinction for which it had been slated. But the cavalrymen found this small comfort, as they believed that if they had been permitted to operate out in front, under real battle conditions, they would have wreaked such havoc as to silence forever the foes of the horse.

However, in March, 1942, the ax fell. Out of a clear sky, the office of Chief of Cavalry, along with the other chiefs of the combat branches, was abolished. The powers of the War Department, under the authority of wartime legislation, then moved swiftly to destroy all our horse cavalry. The great First Cavalry Division, the heart and soul of the mounted service, was dismounted and trained for jungle fighting in the Pacific theater, where it was later acclaimed by Generals MacArthur and Kreuger as the best division in their commands; and Secretary of War Patterson even said he believed it was the best division in the world. The other mounted regiments were converted into vehicular reconnaissance units — and largely wasted. The regiments, as a sop to sentiment, were at least allowed to keep their old names — but that was all.

This drastic action naturally caused deep-seated resentment, which still exists. The cavalrymen considered it unfair and, as later events seemed to prove in the rough terrains of North Africa, Sicily, Italy, and especially in Korea, extremely unwise. That the horse cavalry, to a reasonable number, will some day be revived, all these men firmly believe, once the true facts can be brought out from behind the iron curtain of the Pentagon.

What caused this extreme and sudden action? It was probably a combination of factors. The great successes of the German panzer divisions (which nobody denied) over the good roads in the flat country of northern Europe had their effect on the extremely motor-conscious American public and its tendency to rush *en masse* to extremes. The horse was dead! Long live the motor! Thus reasoned many people who had never tried to cut cross country, between the hard roads, in their shiny, chromium-plated, streamlined pride of the Detroit production line and knew nothing about the use of horses. That there was in-

Generals George Patton and Theodore Roosevelt in
Sicily, August 4, 1943

fluence brought to bear by certain industries which would profit heavily by the production of the enormously expensive tank and other mechanized vehicles is almost certain. Then, there was the ever-eternal green-eyed monster of jealousy which had been aroused in the breasts of the other services, especially among soft and inactive officers behind desks, over the color and glamour attached to the cavalry, over the good times which the officers of that branch enjoyed in their sports at all the cavalry posts, and over the certain indefinable social prestige which the man on horseback, the cavalier, the *hidalgo,* the gentleman, has always had over the man on foot. All these influences combined, and, amidst the excitement at the outbreak of war, managed to eliminate what they called an archaic branch.

All's fair in love and war. And ridicule is the most deadly weapon of all. Any man who can finally make his heart's desire laugh at a serious rival usually has things well in hand. The cavalry probably had as many pompous Colonel Blimps in its ranks as any other service, and against these and the mounted service in general a campaign of ridicule was launched which proved devastating. The cavalry was accused of living in the days of King Arthur — in a dream world, in which it spent its time in happily sliding down canyons on the horses' behind — or inadvertently, occasionally, on the riders'; of galloping headlong to chop at straw-filled dummies with sabers, and of spending its whole time in learning practices which had died with General Custer. The cavalrymen on the march were often greeted with wisecracks such as "Where are your bows and arrows?" or "Hiya, Sir Galahad!" or "What's good for the daily double tomorrow?"

All these quips were probably pretty entertaining at the time to some people but one wonders how funny the officers and men

254

of the infantryized Eighth Cavalry Regiment would have found
them on a gray, cold autumn day in 1950, at Unsan in Korea, in
a completely exposed position where they had been placed by
the blunder of the corps commander. This regiment had been
detached from the First Cavalry Division and taken from the
command of its division commander, a cavalryman under whom
it had fought with great success and distinction, and had been
ordered to support the First ROK (Republic of Korea) Division.

The joker was that this Korean division was not where the
corps commander thought it was, but actually twenty to twenty-
five miles to the rear. The commander of the First Cavalry
Division, solicitous about this severed regiment, had come up
to check on its position, and reported its exposed position to the
corps commander and recommended that it be pulled back at
once; but this was refused over his strenuous protests.

In the meantime two large Chinese columns were advancing
toward the isolated Eighth Cavalry, and although these columns were badly mauled by artillery fire and by attacks from
two battalions of the Fifth Cavalry which had come up, they
kept right on coming. Finally tardy permission was received
that night to withdraw the Eighth Cavalry and the bulk of two
battalions were extricated. But the third battalion, on November 1, 1950, was completely surrounded and five hundred men,
mostly captured, were lost.

Although this disaster largely stemmed from the mistakes of
the corps commander, it certainly could not have happened to
really mobile cavalry, mounted on horses and trained to fight
on foot, as had been the practice of the exterminated U. S. Cavalry. These captured men (those who still survive) have had
nearly three years now in a Communist prison camp to ponder

General George S. Patton, commanding general of the U.S. Third Army, in St. Martin, Austria, rides the horse Favory Africa, one of the famous breed of Lippizzaners of the Spanish Riding School in Vienna, which Adolph Hitler had personally picked out to be presented to Emperor Hirohito of Japan. Circumstances — notably the drive of General Patton's forces into Austria — prevented the gift from reaching the Japanese Emperor and saved the Lippizzaners from capture by the Russians.

over the ridiculous idea of mounted cavalry. And how would the men of other units have felt about these quips at the cavalry when they were nearly decimated by Red guerilla cavalry during the retreat from the Yalu River a little later in the same year? These are a few facts which are not so funny and have been withheld from the American public.

The Twilight

After we entered World War II, there were frantic pleas for horse cavalry from our field commanders in North Africa, Sicily, and Italy; but to no avail — the mounted service was gone, completely disrupted. General George S. Patton later summed up the situation by stating:

> It is the considered opinion, not only of myself but of many other general officers who took their origin from the infantry and artillery, that had we possessed an American cavalry division with pack artillery, in Tunisia and Sicily, not a German would have escaped.

Generals John P. Lucas and Lucian Truscott, who served in Italy, made similar statements after the war, and told of the desperate need they had had in that mountainous land for mounted troops who could move across the rugged countryside. In the Pacific theater, General Jonathan Wainwright said, after his return from captivity:

> The 26th Cavalry [a regiment of Filipinos officered almost entirely by Americans] was the only Regular Army Unit available to me, so I used it very extensively to cover my withdrawal [from Lingayen Gulf to Bataan, 140 miles]. This it did in a masterful and heroic manner. Without it, I doubt if the withdrawal of my Corps would have been so successfully accomplished.
>
> As the last Senior Commander to employ Cavalry against an armed enemy, perhaps my opinion of the value of Mounted Cavalry is entitled to some consideration.

But evidently General Wainwright's opinion, as well as that of the others, was of no value, for the War Department went merrily on, after the war, to sell all the cavalry horses, all the cavalry equipment, and all the cavalry posts, so as utterly to extinguish its existence. And this despite General Staff Intelligence Bulletins (kept secret from the public) that the Soviets had used horse cavalry to great advantage during the recent war; so much so that the mechanized German army was forced to turn back to the horse, which it had previously eliminated, and to form, from 1943 to 1945, six mounted cavalry divisions and two cavalry corps to cope with the fifty Russian cavalry divisions in the field. Today, the Russians are believed to have some twenty-five mounted divisions against our none; and we have reaped part of the whirlwind in the Korean stalemate.

To sum up, as simply as possible for the lay reader, the case for the mounted cavalry: wars flow over all kinds of terrain, in all kinds of weather, and an alert enemy will try to fight in the kind best suited to his resources. Korea is an example of this. And there are many other areas in the world where the country is too rough and rugged for anything on wheels or treads but where mounted cavalry and pack trains can operate with ease. Mexico, which can be called our soft underbelly, is an example of that. Mounted cavalry can always supply many needed reconnaissance reports which the Air Force can not furnish at night or in bad weather, and which the motorized armored scouting units now in use can not supply when they are blocked on the roads or unable to move across country. No foe within range can hide from cavalry, in fair or foul weather, by day or night, on or off the roads. To quote General Patton again:

> Against motorized and mechanized armies, vehicular reconnaissance is adequate. If we were to fight opponents who depended on animal transportation or their feet, horse reconnaissance would be necessary.

The exponents of mounted cavalry are reasonable in their requests. They only ask that a small cadre which can be expanded if necessary, one cavalry division, be remounted — the splendid

First Cavalry Division, first in Manila and first in Tokyo, which has added further luster to its laurels in Korea. It still mourns for its horses; and what a huzza would resound from its members and from all dyed-in-the-wool horse lovers which would be echoed in Valhalla by the spirits of all American cavalrymen

U.S. Army Photograph

Unconquered! The return of the last command of U.S. mounted trops in warfare. Brigadier General Clinton A. Pierce, on the right, who commanded the 26th cavalry when it covered the retreat to Bataan, lands in Hawaii after years spent in a Japanese prison camp.

U.S. Army Photograph

General Jonathan Wainwright, at Fort Sam Houston, Texas, on January 16, 1947, has just received back the sword which he surrendered at Corregidor.

from Casimir Pulaski to George S. Patton. The sands are running out. The valuable abilities of the experienced officers and men of this division will be lost forever in a few more years. The Achilles' heel of our army today is its lack of horse cavalry — and it may well prove just as fatal.

One basic and immutable truth stands out through all our wars. Sometimes our commanders have had to learn it the hard way:

There is no substitute for cavalry!

Bibliography

Adam, F. Colburn, *The Story of a Trooper.* New York, 1865.

Adams, Charles Francis, "Washington and Cavalry." *Studies Military and Diplomatic.* New York, 1911.

Allgemeines — Taschenbuch, Berlin, 1784.

American Battle Painting. National Gallery of Art, Washington, and Museum of Modern Art, New York, 1944.

American State Papers, Military Affairs. Washington, 1789–1838.

Appleton's Cyclopaedia of American Biography. New York, 1887.

Armes, G. A., *Ups and Downs of an Army Officer.* Washington, 1900.

Army Almanac. Washington, 1950.

Army and Navy Journal. Files: 1863–1942.

Avirett, James B., *The Memoirs of Turner Ashby and His Compeers.* Baltimore, 1867.

Baird, Maj. G. W., "General Miles's Indian Campaigns." *Century Magazine.* July, 1891.

Balch, Thomas, *The French in America.* Philadelphia, 1891.

Battles and Leaders of the Civil War. Robert Underwood Johnson and Clarence Clough Buel, eds. 4 volumes. New York, 1888.

Bauer, Frederic Gilbert, "Notes on the Use of Cavalry in the American Revolution." *Cavalry Journal.* March-April, 1938.

Baylies, Francis, *Narrative of Maj. Gen. Wool's Campaign in Mexico.* Albany, 1851.

Beers, Henry Putney, "The Army and the Oregon Trail to 1846." *Pacific Northwest Quarterly.* October, 1937.

Benham, H. W., *Recollections of Mexico and the Battle of Buena Vista.* Boston, 1871.

Bibliography

Bennett, James Augustus, *Forts and Forays*. Albuquerque, New Mexico, 1948.

Biddle, Ellen McGowan, *Reminiscences of a Soldier's Wife*. Philadelphia, 1907.

Blackford, W. W., *War Years with Jeb Stuart*. New York, 1945.

Bonsted, Capt. F. T., *The 11th Cavalry*. Monterey, California, 1923.

Bourke, Capt. John G., *An Apache Campaign*. New York, 1886.

———, "General Crook in the Indian Country." *Century Magazine*. March, 1891.

———, *Mackenzie's Last Fight with the Cheyennes*. Governor's Island, New York, 1890.

———, *On the Border with Crook*. New York, 1891.

"Bourke on the Southwest," Lansing R. Bloom, ed. *New Mexico Historical Review*. January, 1934.

Boyd, Mrs. Orsemus Bronson, *Cavalry Life in Tent and Field*. New York, 1894.

Brackett, G. Albert, *General Lane's Brigade in Central Mexico*. Cincinnati, 1854.

———, *History of the United States Cavalry*. New York, 1865.

Bradford, Gamaliel, *Confederate Portraits*. Boston, 1914.

Brady, Cyrus Townsend *Indian Fights and Fighters*. New York, 1923.

Brandt, John H., *The 5th Cavalry*. Los Angeles, 1938.

Brininstool, E. A., *A Trooper with Custer*. Columbus, Ohio, 1925.

Brooks, Van Wyck, *The World of Washington Irving*. New York, 1944.

Byrne, P. E., *Soldiers of the Plains*. New York, 1926.

Carleton, James Henry, *The Battle of Buena Vista*. New York, 1848.

Carrington, F. C., *My Army Life and the Fort Phil. Kearny Massacre*. Philadelphia, 1910.

Carter, Capt. R. G., *The Old Sergeant's Story*. New York, 1926.

———, *On The Border With Mackenzie*. Washington, 1935.

Carter, Maj. Gen. William Harding, "Early History of American Cavalry." *Cavalry Journal*. January, 1925.

Bibliography

————, *From Yorktown to Santiago with the Sixth U. S. Cavalry.* Baltimore, 1900.

————, *Horses, Saddles and Bridles.* Baltimore, 1902.

Cashin, Hershel V., *The 9th and 10th Cavalry.* New York, 1899.

Catlin, George, *North American Indians.* 2 volumes. Philadelphia, 1913.

Cavalry Journal. Files: 1888–1942.

Cavalry, Light Infantry, and Rifle Tactics. Washington, 1834.

Cavalry Tactics. Washington, 1841.

Centennial of the U.S.M.A. at West Point, New York. 2 volumes. Washington, 1904.

Century Magazine. Files: 1870–1900.

Cook, James H., *50 Years on the Old Frontier.* New Haven, 1925.

Cooke, Philip St. George, *Cavalry Tactics.* Washington, 1861.

————, *Conquest of New Mexico and Arizona.* New York, 1878.

————, "One Day's Work of a Captain of Dragoons." *Magazine of American History.* July, 1887.

————, *Scenes and Adventures in the Army.* Philadelphia, 1857.

Corle, Edwin, *The Gila, River of the Southwest.* New York, 1951.

Crimmins, Col. M. L., "General Mackenzie and Fort Concho." *West Texas Historical Association Year Book.* 1934.

————, "He Might Have Been an Emperor." *Dallas Morning News.* January 3, 1937.

————, "Our Army Families: The Ords." Typescript, n.d.

Crowninshield, Benjamin W., "Cavalry in Virginia During The War of the Rebellion." *Civil and Mexican Wars 1861, 1848.* Papers of the Military Historical Society of Massachusetts, Volume XIII. Boston, 1913.

Cullum, G. W., *Bibliographical Register of the Officers and Graduates of the U. S. Military Academy, 1802–1890.* Boston, 1891.

Custer Battlefield, The, National Park Service. Washington, 1949.

Custer, Elizabeth B., *Boots and Saddles.* New York, 1885.

————, *Following the Guidon.* New York, 1890.

————, *Tenting on the Plains.* New York, 1887.

Bibliography

Custer Fight, The: Captain F. W. Benteen's Story of the Little Big Horn, June 25–26, 1876. Arranged by E. A. Brininstool. Hollywood, 1940.

Custer, Gen. G. A., *My Life on the Plains.* New York, 1874.

Dana, Charles A., *The United States Illustrated.* New York, 1855.

Darrow, Pierce, *Cavalry Tactics.* Hartford, 1822.

Davis, Richard Harding, *Cuba in War Time.* New York, 1898.

Deibert, Ralph C., *History of 3rd U. S. Cavalry.* Philadelphia, n.d.

Dennison, Col. George T., *A History of Cavalry from the Earliest Times.* London, 1913.

Depredations on the Frontiers of Texas — 1874. 43d Con. 1st Sess. H. of R. Exec. Doc. No. 257.

Dictionary of American Biography. 21 volumes. New York, 1928–1944.

Dictionary of National Biography. Volume LV. London, 1898.

Dobie, J. Frank, *Tongues of the Monte.* New York, 1935.

Dodge, Richard Irving, *Our Wild Indians.* Hartford, 1882.

————, *The Plains of the Great West.* New York, 1877.

Dorst, John H., "Ranald Slidell Mackenzie." *Twentieth Annual Reunion of the Association of Graduates, U. S. Military Academy, 1889.* East Saginaw, Michigan, 1889.

Downey, Fairfax, *Indian-Fighting Army.* New York, 1941.

Dupuy, Col. R. Ernest, *Men of West Point.* New York, 1951.

Dustin, Fred., *The Custer Tragedy.* Ann Arbor, 1939.

Ellis, Edward S., *The Indian Wars of the United States.* Grand Rapids, 1892.

Emory, Lieut. Col. W. H., *Notes of a Military Reconnaissance, from Ft. Leavenworth, in Missouri, to San Diego, in California.* (Also contains Lieut. Col. P. St. G. Cooke's report to Gen. Stephen Kearny and the journal of Capt. A. R. Johnston, 1st Dragoons.) Washington, 1848.

Faust, Karl Irving, *Campaigning in the Philippines.* San Francisco, 1899.

Fee, Chester Anders, *Chief Joseph.* New York, 1936.

Bibliography

Forsyth, Brevet Brig. Gen. George A., *The Story of the Soldier.* New York, 1900.

——, *Thrilling Days in Army Life.* New York, 1900.

Foster, John W., *Diplomatic Memories.* 2 volumes. New York, 1909.

Fougera, Katherine Gibson, *With Custer's Cavalry.* Caldwell, Idaho, 1940.

Fourth Cavalry, U. S. A. 1855–1920. Fort Meade, South Dakota, 1930.

Frank Leslie's Pictorial History of the War of 1861, New York, 1862.

Freeman, Douglas Southall, *Lee's Lieutenants.* 3 volumes. New York, 1942–1944.

——, *R. E. Lee.* 4 volumes. New York, 1934–1935.

French, Hon. Edward Gerald, *Good-bye to Boot and Saddle.* London, 1951.

Frontier Times, Bandera, Texas. Files: 1930–

Frost, John, *Pictorial History of Mexico and the Mexican War.* Philadelphia, 1848.

Ganoe, William Addleman, *The History of the United States Army.* New York, 1942.

Gardner, Robert E., *American Arms and Arms Makers.* Columbus, Ohio, 1938.

Glass, Edward L., *History of the 10th Cavalry.* Tucson, Arizona, 1921.

Glazier, Willard, *Three Years in the Federal Cavalry.* New York, 1873.

Godfrey, Capt. E. S., "Custer's Last Battle." *Century Magazine.* January, 1892.

Graham, Lieut. Col. W. A., *The Story of the Little Big Horn.* New York, 1926.

Grandmaison, Major General de, *A Treatise on the Military Service of Light Horse.* Philadelphia, 1777.

Grant, U. S., *Personal Memoirs.* 2 volumes. New York, 1892.

Gray, Alonzo, *Cavalry Tactics.* Fort Leavenworth, 1910.

Greely, Maj. Gen. A. W., *Reminiscences of Adventure and Service.* New York, 1927.

Bibliography

Greer, James Kimmins, *Colonel Jack Hays*. New York, 1952.

Griffin, Martin I. J., *Stephen Moylan*. Philadelphia, 1909.

Grinnell, George Bird, *The Fighting Cheyennes*. New York, 1915.

Haberly, Lloyd, *Pursuit of the Horizon: A Life of George Catlin*. New York, 1948.

Hagedorn, Hermann, *Leonard Wood: A Biography*. New York, 1931.

Hamersly, Thomas H. S., *Complete Regular Army Register of the United States: For One Hundred Years (1779–1879)*. Washington, 1880.

Handy, Mary Olivia, *History of Fort Sam Houston*. San Antonio, 1951.

Harmon, George D., *The U. S. Indian Policy in Texas, 1845–1860*. Lehigh University, Bethlehem, Pennsylvania, 1931.

Harper's Magazine. Files: 1850–1900.

Harper's Pictorial History of the Great Rebellion. New York, 1866–1868.

Harper's Weekly. Files: 1857–1900.

H Book of Harvard Athletics 1852–1922. John A. Blanchard, ed. Cambridge, Massachusetts, 1923.

Heitman, F. B., *Historical Register and Dictionary of the U. S. Army*. 2 volumes. Washington, 1903.

Henry, Robert Selph, *"First With The Most" Forrest*. Indianapolis, 1944.

Hershberger, H. R., *The Horseman*. New York, 1844.

Hicks, Maj. James E., *Notes on United States Ordnance*. Volume I. Mount Vernon, New York, 1940.

Hildreth, Henry, *Dragoon Campaigns to the Rocky Mountains*. New York, 1836.

History and Pictorial Review, Sixth Cavalry. Baton Rouge, Louisiana, 1941.

History 5th U. S. Cavalry 1855 to 1927. Fort Clark, Texas, 1927.

Hodge, F. W., *Handbook on American Indians*. 2 volumes. Washington, 1910.

Hoffman, Charles Fenno, *A Winter in the West*. 2 volumes. New York, 1835.

Bibliography

Holland, C. F., *Morgan and His Raiders*. New York, 1943.

Howard, O. O., *My Life and Experiences Among Our Hostile Indians*. Hartford, 1907.

Hubbard, James Milton, *Notes of a Private With Forrest*. St. Louis, 1911.

Hughes, John T., *Doniphan's Expedition*. Cincinnati, 1847.

Irving, Washington, *A Tour on the Prairies*. Philadelphia, 1835.

Jenks, E. A., *Cavalry Exercise*. Portland, Maine, 1801.

Johnston, Charles H. L., *Famous Cavalry Leaders*. Boston, 1908.

Johnston, William Preston, *The Life of Gen. Albert Sidney Johnston*. New York, 1880.

Journal of Colonel Dodge's Expedition from Fort Gibson to the Pawnee Pict Village. Sen. Exec. Doc., No. 1, 23rd Con. 2nd Sess. 1834.

Journal of the Military Service Institution of the United States. Files: 1879–1916.

Kearny, Gen. Philip, "Service with the French Troops in Africa." *The Magazine of History*. Extra No. 22, 1913.

Kearny, Thomas, *General Philip Kearny, Battle Soldier of Five Wars*. New York, 1937.

Keim, De Beusseville Randolph, *Sheridan's Troopers on the Border*. New York, 1885.

King, Capt. Charles, *Campaigning with Crook*. New York, 1890.

———, "Custer's Last Battle." *Harper's New Monthly Magazine*. July, 1890.

Kuhlman, Charles, *Legend into History: the Custer Mystery*. Harrisburg, Pennsylvania, 1951.

Lambert, Maj. Joseph I., *100 Years with the 2nd Cavalry*. Topeka, Kansas, 1939.

Lane, Lydia Spencer, *I Married a Soldier*. Philadelphia, 1893.

Larson, James, *Sergeant Larson of the 4th Cavalry*. San Antonio, 1935.

Lauzun, Memoire of the Duc de. Translated by E. Jules Miras. New York, 1912.

Bibliography

Lee, Henry, *Memoirs of the War in the Southern Department of the United States.* 2 volumes. Philadelphia, 1812.

Lefferts, Lieut. Charles M., *Uniforms of the American, British, French, and German Armies in the War of the American Revolution, 1775–1783.* New York, 1926.

Leslie's Illustrated Weekly Newspaper. Files: 1855–1900.

Leslie's Official History of the Spanish-American War. Washington, 1899.

Lewis, James O., *Aboriginal Port-Folio.* Philadelphia, 1835.

Lockwood, Frank C. *The Apache Indians.* New York, 1938.

Lodge, Henry Cabot, *The Story of the Revolution.* New York, 1898.

Longstreet, James, *From Manassas to Appomattox.* Philadelphia, 1896.

Loring, W. W., *A Confederate Soldier in Egypt.* New York, 1884.

Lossing, Benson J., *Pictorial Field Book of the Civil War.* 3 volumes. Hartford, 1874.

——, *Pictorial Field Book of the Revolution.* 2 volumes. New York, 1852.

——, *Pictorial Field Book of the War of 1812.* New York, 1868.

Lowe, Percival G., *Five Years a Dragoon.* Kansas City, Missouri, 1906.

Luce, Capt. Edward S., *Keogh, Comanche, and Custer.* Dedham, Massachusetts, 1939.

Lytle, Andrew Nelson, *Bedford Forrest.* London, 1939.

March of the Mounted Riflemen . . . from Ft. Leavenworth to Ft. Vancouver, May to October 1849. Raymond W. Settle, ed. Glendale, California, 1940.

Marcy, Randolph B., *Border Reminiscences.* New York, 1872.

Marquis, Thomas B., *A Warrior Who Fought Custer.* Minneapolis, 1931.

Marshall, John, *Life of George Washington.* 5 volumes. Philadelphia, 1804–1807.

Maury, Dabney Herndon, *Recollections of a Virginian in the Mexican, Indian, and Civil Wars.* New York, 1894.

Bibliography

McClellan, George B., *Regulations and Instructions for the Field Service of the U. S. Cavalry in Time of War, 1861.* Philadelphia, 1861.

———, *Report on the Organization and Campaigns of the Army of the Potomac.* New York, 1864.

McConnell, H. H., *Five Years a Cavalryman.* Jacksboro, Texas, 1889.

McConnell, J. C., *West Texas Frontier.* Palo Pinto, Texas, 1939.

McCrady, Edward, *The History of South Carolina in the Revolution, 1780–1783.* New York, 1902.

McDonald, Capt. William N., *A History of the Laurel Brigade.* Baltimore, 1907.

McGee, Joseph H., *Story of the Grand River Country.* Gallatin, Missouri, 1909.

Mellor, William Bancroft, *Patton: Fighting Man.* New York, 1946.

Merritt, Gen. Wesley, *Thirty Years of Army Life on the Border.* New York, 1866.

———, "Three Indian Campaigns." *Harper's New Monthly Magazine.* April, 1890.

Miles, Gen. Nelson A., *Personal Recollections and Observations.* New York, 1896.

Montross, Lynn, *Rag, Tag and Bobtail.* New York, 1952.

Moore, James, *Kilpatrick and Our Cavalry.* New York, 1865.

Nebel, Carl, and Kendall, George Wilkins, *The War Between the United States and Mexico Illustrated.* New York, 1851.

Niles National Register. Files: 1811–1849.

Nye, W. S., *Carbine and Lance, The Story of Old Fort Sill.* Norman, Oklahoma, 1937.

Order of Indian Wars of the United States, Proceedings. 1911–

Pageant of America. 15 volumes. New Haven, 1925–1929.

Pariset, Nicholas, *The American Trooper's Pocket Companion.* Trenton, 1793.

Parker, James, *The Old Army: Memories, 1872–1918.* Philadelphia, 1929.

Pelzer, Louis, *Marches of the Dragoons in the Mississippi Valley.* Iowa City, 1917.

271

———, *The Prairie Logbooks*. Chicago, 1943.

Photographic History of the Civil War. Volume IV. *The Cavalry*. Theo. F. Rodenbough, ed. New York, 1911.

Posts of the Military Division of the Missouri Commanded by Lieut. Gen. P. H. Sheridan. Chicago, 1876.

Powell, E. Alexander, *The Road to Glory*. New York, 1915.

Pratt, Fletcher, "The Man Who Got There First." *Military Engineer*. May, 1948.

———, *A Short History of the Civil War*. New York, 1952.

Prentice, Royal A., "The Rough Riders." *New Mexico Historical Review*. October, 1951, and January, 1952.

Preston, John Hyde, *A Short History of the American Revolution*. New York, 1952.

Preston, N. D., *History of the Tenth Regiment of Cavalry, New York State Volunteers*. New York, 1892.

Price, George F., *Across The Continent with the 5th Cavalry*. New York, 1883.

Read, T. Buchanan, *Sheridan's Ride*. Philadelphia, 1891.

Reavis, L. V., *Life and Military Services of Gen. William Selby Harney*. St. Louis, 1878.

Record of Engagements with Hostile Indians within the Military Division of the Missouri from 1868–1882. Chicago, 1882.

Reeve, Frank D., "Frederick E. Phelps: A Soldier's Memoirs." *New Mexico Historical Review*. July, 1950.

Reid, Capt. Mayne, "A Dashing Dragoon." *The Magazine of History*. Extra No. 22, 1913.

Reid, Samuel C., *The Scouting Expeditions of McCulloch's Texas Rangers*. Philadelphia, 1847.

Remington, Frederick, *Crooked Trails*. New York, 1899.

———, *Done in the Open*. New York, 1903.

———, *Drawings*. New York, 1897.

———, *Pony Tracks*. New York, 1895.

———, *Remington's Frontier Sketches*. New York, 1898.

"Report on the Expedition of Dragoons under Colonel Henry Dodge,

Bibliography

To the Rocky Mountains in 1835." *American State Papers, Military Affairs*. Vol. VI, No. 624, 24th Con., 1st Sess. 1835.

Reports of the Secretary of War. 1789–1942.

Richardson, Albert D., *Beyond the Mississippi*. Hartford, 1867.

Richardson, Rupert Norval, *The Comanche Barrier to South Plains Settlement*. Glendale, California, 1933.

Richardson, William H., *Journal*. New York, 1848.

Rippy, J. Fred, *The United States and Mexico*. New York, 1926.

Rister, Carl Coke, *Border Command: General Phil Sheridan in the West*. Norman, Oklahoma, 1944.

——, *Robert E. Lee in Texas*. Norman, Oklahoma, 1946.

——, *The Southwestern Frontier*. Cleveland, 1928.

Robinson, Fayette, *The Army of the United States*. 2 volumes. Philadelphia, 1848.

Robinson, Sara T. D., *Kansas, Its Interior and Exterior Life*. Boston, 1856.

Rodenbough, Theo. F., compiler. *From Everglade to Cañon with the Second Dragoons*. New York, 1875.

Rodenbough, Theo. F., and Haskin, William L., *The Army of the United States*. New York, 1896.

Roosevelt, Theodore, *The Rough Riders*. New York, 1899.

Ruxton, George Frederick, *Life in the Far West*. Norman, Oklahoma, 1951.

Schreyvogel, Charles, *My Bunky and Others*. New York, 1909.

——, *Souvenir Album of Painting*. Hoboken, 1907.

Second United States Cavalry, 1836–1936. Fort Riley, Kansas, 1936.

Sheridan, Gen. Philip Henry, *Personal Memoirs*. 2 volumes. New York, 1888.

Sherman, Gen. W. T., *Memoirs*. 2 volumes. New York, 1891.

Smith, Justin H., *The War with Mexico*. 2 volumes. New York, 1919.

Southwestern Historical Quarterly. Files: 1897–

Spaulding, Col. Oliver Lyman, *The United States Army in War and Peace*. New York, 1937.

Stanley, Maj. Gen. D. S., *Personal Memoirs*. Cambridge, Massachusetts, 1917.

Bibliography

Steele, James W., *Frontier Army Sketches*. Chicago, 1883.

Steele, Mathew Forney, *American Campaigns*. Washington, 1943.

Stong, Phil., *Horses and Americans*. New York, 1939.

Summerhays, Martha, *Vanished Arizona: Recollections of the Army Life of a New England Woman*. Salem, Massachusetts, 1911.

Swiggett, Howard, *The Rebel Raider*. Indianapolis, 1934.

Sword Exercises, Drill, and Evolutions for the Cavalry. Philadelphia, 1812.

Taft, Robert, "The Pictorial Record of the Old West: Custer's Last Stand." *The Kansas Historical Quarterly*. November, 1946.

Texas, A Guide to the Lone Star State. Federal Writers Project, WPA. New York, 1940.

Thomason, John W., *Jeb Stuart*. New York, 1930.

Todd, Frederick P., *Soldiers of the American Army, 1775–1941*. New York, 1941.

Tompkins, Frank, *Chasing Villa*. Harrisburg, Pennsylvania, 1934.

Tone, William Theobald Wolfe, *School of Cavalry*. Georgetown, Virginia, 1824.

Trobriand, Régis, Comte de, *Vie Militaire dans le Dakota*. Paris, 1926.

Tuttle, Charles Richard, *History of the Border Wars of Two Centuries*. Madison, Wisconsin, 1874.

Uncle Sam's Camels, Lewis Burt Lesley, ed. Cambridge, Massachusetts, 1929.

Uniform of the Army of the United States 1774 to 1889. Quartermaster Corps. Washington, 1894.

United States Military Magazine, 1840.

Upton, Emory, *The Military Policy of the United States*. Washington, 1912.

Vaill, Dudley Landon, *The County Regiment. A Sketch of the Second Regiment of Connecticut Volunteer Heavy Artillery, Originally the Nineteenth Volunteer Infantry, in the Civil War*. Litchfield County (Connecticut) University Club, 1908.

Vaill, Theodore F., *History of the Second Connecticut Volunteer*

Heavy Artillery, Originally the Nineteenth Connecticut Volunteers. Winsted, Connecticut, 1868.

Van de Water, Frederic F., *Glory-Hunter: A Life of General Custer.* Indianapolis, 1934.

Vestal, Stanley, *Sitting Bull.* Boston, 1932.

Viele, Mrs. E. L., *"Following the Drum": A Glimpse of Frontier life.* New York, 1858.

Wagner, Lieut. Col. Arthur L., *The United States Army and Navy.* Akron, Ohio, 1899.

Wagner, Glendolin Damon, *Old Neutriment.* Boston, 1934.

Wainwright, Jonathan M., *General Wainwright's Story.* New York, 1946.

Walton, William, *The Army and Navy of the United States.* Boston, 1900.

Washington, George. *Writings of George Washington,* Jared Sparks, ed. 12 volumes. Boston, 1834–1837.

Webb, Walter Prescott, *The Great Plains.* Boston, 1931.

Wellman, Paul I., *Death in the Desert.* New York, 1935.

———, *Death on the Prairie.* New York, 1934.

Westermeier, Clifford P., "Teddy's Terrors: The New Mexican Volunteers of 1898." *New Mexico Historical Review.* April, 1952.

White, Anthony Walton, *The Military System for the New Jersey Cavalry.* New Brunswick, 1793.

Wilson, Maj. Gen. James H., "The Cavalry of the Army of the Potomac." *Civil and Mexican Wars 1861, 1848.* Papers of the Military Historical Society of Massachusetts. Volume XIII. Boston, 1913.

Wilson, James Harrison, *Under the Old Flag.* 2 volumes. New York, 1912.

Wyeth, John Allan, *Life of General Nathan Bedford Forrest.* New York, 1899.

Young, Col. Bennett H., *The Battle of the Thames.* Louisville, 1903.

———, *Confederate Wizards of the Saddle.* Boston, 1914.

Zogbaum, Rufus Fairchild, *Horse, Foot, and Dragoons.* New York, 1888.